Teach Yourself VISUALLY™

Mac OS® X Tiger™

Visual

by Erick Tejkowski

WILEY

Wiley Publishing, Inc.

Teach Yourself VISUALLY™
Mac OS® X Tiger™

Published by
Wiley Publishing, Inc.
111 River Street
Hoboken, NJ 07030-5774

Published simultaneously in Canada

Library of Congress Control Number: 2005923188

ISBN-13: 978-0-7645-7698-0

ISBN-10: 0-7645-7698-4

Manufactured in the United States of America

10 9 8 7 6 5 4 3 2

Trademark Acknowledgments

Contact Us

For general information on our other products and services please contact our Customer Care Department within the U.S. at 800-762-2974, outside the U.S. at 317-572-3993 or fax 317-572-4002.

For technical support please visit www.wiley.com/techsupport.

Wiley Publishing, Inc.

Sales

Contact Wiley
at (800) 762-2974 or
fax (317) 572-4002.

Praise for Visual Books

"Like a lot of other people, I understand things best when I see them visually. Your books really make learning easy and life more fun."

John T. Frey (Cadillac, MI)

"I have quite a few of your Visual books and have been very pleased with all of them. I love the way the lessons are presented!"

Mary Jane Newman (Yorba Linda, CA)

"I just purchased my third Visual book (my first two are dog-eared now!), and, once again, your product has surpassed my expectations.

Tracey Moore (Memphis, TN)

"I am an avid fan of your Visual books. If I need to learn anything, I just buy one of your books and learn the topic it in no time. Wonders! I have even trained my friends to give me Visual books as gifts."

Illona Bergstrom (Aventura, FL)

"Thank you for making it so clear. I appreciate it. I will buy many more Visual books."

J.P. Sangdong (North York, Ontario, Canada)

"I have several books from the Visual series and have always found them to be valuable resources."

Stephen P. Miller (Ballston Spa, NY)

"Thank you for the wonderful books you produce. It wasn't until I was an adult that I discovered how I learn – visually. Nothing compares to Visual books. I love the simple layout. I can just grab a book and use it at my computer, lesson by lesson. And I understand the material! You really know the way I think and learn. Thanks so much!"

Stacey Han (Avondale, AZ)

"I absolutely admire your company's work. Your books are terrific. The format is perfect, especially for visual learners like me. Keep them coming!"

Frederick A. Taylor, Jr. (New Port Richey, FL)

"I have several of your Visual books and they are the best I have ever used."

Stanley Clark (Crawfordville, FL)

"I bought my first Teach Yourself VISUALLY book last month. Wow. Now I want to learn everything in this easy format!"

Tom Vial (New York, NY)

"Thank you, thank you, thank you...for making it so easy for me to break into this high-tech world. I now own four of your books. I recommend them to anyone who is a beginner like myself."

Gay O'Donnell (Calgary, Alberta, Canada)

"I write to extend my thanks and appreciation for your books. They are clear, easy to follow, and straight to the point. Keep up the good work! I bought several of your books and they are just right! No regrets! I will always buy your books because they are the best."

Seward Kollie (Dakar, Senegal)

"Compliments to the chef!! Your books are extraordinary! Or, simply put, extra-ordinary, meaning way above the rest! THANKYOU THANKYOU THANKYOU! I buy them for friends, family, and colleagues."

Christine J. Manfrin (Castle Rock, CO)

"What fantastic teaching books you have produced! Congratulations to you and your staff. You deserve the Nobel Prize in Education in the Software category. Thanks for helping me understand computers."

Bruno Tonon (Melbourne, Australia)

"Over time, I have bought a number of your 'Read Less - Learn More' books. For me, they are THE way to learn anything easily. I learn easiest using your method of teaching."

José A. Mazón (Cuba, NY)

"I am an avid purchaser and reader of the Visual series, and they are the greatest computer books I've seen. The Visual books are perfect for people like myself who enjoy the computer, but want to know how to use it more efficiently. Your books have definitely given me a greater understanding of my computer, and have taught me to use it more effectively. Thank you very much for the hard work, effort, and dedication that you put into this series."

Alex Diaz (Las Vegas, NV)

Credits

Project Editor
Tim Borek

Acquisitions Editor
Jody Lefevere

Product Development Manager
Lindsay Sandman

Copy Editor
Kim Heusel

Technical Editor
Dennis Cohen

Editorial Manager
Robyn Siesky

Manufacturing
Allan Conley
Linda Cook
Paul Gilchrist
Jennifer Guynn

Illustrators
Steven Amory
Matthew Bell
Ronda David-Burroughs
Cheryl Grubbs
Sean Johanessen
Jacob Mansfield
Rita Marley
Tyler Roloff
Diane Staver

Book Design
Kathie Rickard

Production Coordinator
Maridee Ennis

Layout
Beth Brooks
Jennifer Heleine
LeAndra Hosier
Amanda Spagnuolo

Screen Artist
Jill Proll

Proofreader
Arielle Mennelle

Quality Control
Laura Albert
Susan Moritz

Indexer
Johnna VanHoose

Special Help
Marylouise Wiack

Vice President and Executive Group Publisher
Richard Swadley

Vice President and Publisher
Barry Pruett

Composition Director
Debbie Stailey

About the Author

Erick Tejkowski is a writer and developer who lives near St. Louis, Missouri, with his wife, Maria, and his two children, Mercedes and Leopold. He has written numerous Mac-related books and articles, including *Mac OS X Panther: Top 100 Simplified Tips and Tricks* and *REALbasic For Dummies*. His articles have appeared in magazines like *MacWorld*, *MacTech*, and *MacAddict*.

Author's Acknowledgments

A special thanks goes to Tim Borek, project editor. Without his excellent advice and keen eye for detail, this book would not be what it is. Additionally, extended recognition goes to Jody Lefevere for her support. Thanks also to Dennis Cohen for providing his technical expertise as the Technical Editor and to Kim Heusel for his help as copy editor.

TABLE OF CONTENTS

Mac OS X Tiger Fundamentals

Mastering the Finder

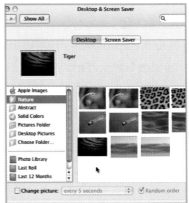

chapter 3

Customizing Tiger with the System Preferences

chapter 4

Completing Everyday Tasks

TABLE OF CONTENTS

Working with Images

Listening to Music

TABLE OF CONTENTS

chapter 9 — Connecting to Other Machines on a Network

chapter 10 — Utilities

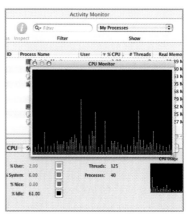

chapter 11

Connecting Peripherals to a Mac

chapter 12

Troubleshooting Mac Problems

HOW TO USE THIS BOOK

How to Use This Teach Yourself VISUALLY Book

Do you look at the pictures in a book or newspaper before anything else on a page? Would you rather see an image instead of read about how to do something? Search no further. This book is for you. Opening *Teach Yourself VISUALLY Mac OS X Tiger* allows you to read less and learn more about Tiger.

Who Needs This Book

This book is for a reader who has never used this particular technology or software application. It is also for more-computer-literate individuals who want to expand their knowledge of the different features that Mac OS X Tiger has to offer. We assume you have either never used Mac OS X before or have worked with earlier versions but want to know about what is new in the latest version.

Book Organization

Teach Yourself VISUALLY Mac OS X Tiger has 12 chapters.

Chapter Organization

This book consists of sections, all listed in the book's table of contents. A *section* is a set of steps that show you how to complete a specific computer task.

Each section, usually contained on two facing pages, has an introduction to the task at hand, a set of full-color screen shots and steps that walk you through the task, and a set of tips. This format allows you to quickly look at a topic of interest and learn it instantly.

Chapters group together three or more sections with a common theme. A chapter may also contain pages that give you the background information needed to understand the sections in a chapter.

What You Need to Use This Book

Some sections of this book feature additional software, such as iMovie, which is not included with Mac OS X Tiger. If your Mac had Tiger installed when purchased new, it may already have iLife installed.

Using the Mouse

This book uses the following conventions to describe the actions you perform when using the mouse:

Click

Press your mouse button (the left button, if you have a two-button mouse) once. You generally click your mouse on something to select something on the screen.

Double-click

Press your mouse button (the left button, if you have a two-button mouse) twice. Double-clicking something on the computer screen generally opens whatever item you have double-clicked.

Control-click

Press your mouse button while holding down the Control key (Control) on your keyboard. When you Control-click something on the computer screen, the program displays a contextual menu containing commands specific to the selected item. If you are using a two-button mouse, a right-click is equivalent to a Control-click.

Click and Drag, and Release the Mouse

Move your mouse pointer and hover it over an item on the screen. Press and hold down the mouse button. Now, move the mouse to where you want to place the item and then release the button. You use this method to move an item from one area of the computer screen to another.

The Conventions in This Book

A number of typographic and layout styles have been used throughout *Teach Yourself VISUALLY Mac OS X Tiger* to distinguish different types of information.

Bold

Bold type represents the names of commands and options with which you interact. Bold type also indicates text and numbers that you must type into a dialog box or window.

Italics

Italic words introduce a new term and are followed by a definition.

Numbered Steps

You must perform the instructions in numbered steps in order to successfully complete a section and achieve the final results.

Bulleted Steps

These steps point out various optional features. You do not have to perform these steps; they simply give additional information about a feature.

Indented Text

Indented text tells you what the program does in response to your following a numbered step. For example, if you click a certain menu command, a dialog box may appear, or a window may open. Indented text may also tell you what the final result is when you follow a set of numbered steps.

Notes

Notes give additional information. They may describe special conditions that may occur during an operation. They may warn you of a situation that you want to avoid, for example, the loss of data. A note may also cross-reference a related area of the book. A cross-reference may guide you to another chapter, or another section within the current chapter.

Icons and Buttons

Icons and buttons are graphical representations within the text. They show you exactly what you need to click to perform a step.

 You can easily identify the tips in any section by looking for the TIPS icon. Tips offer additional information, including tips, hints, and tricks. You can use the TIPS information to go beyond what you have learned in the steps.

1

Mac OS X Tiger Fundamentals

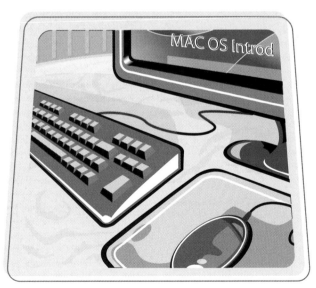

The Macintosh operating system, often abbreviated Mac OS, is the software that makes your Macintosh computer run. It gives you the ability to work with a mouse, a keyboard, windows, files, and can even offer help when you run into trouble.

Mac OS Introduction

The Macintosh Operating System is a collection of programs that makes your computer run. It is responsible for opening and saving files, displaying graphics on the screen, printing documents on a printer, and accepting input from the mouse and keyboard. The Mac OS is what makes your computer work for you.

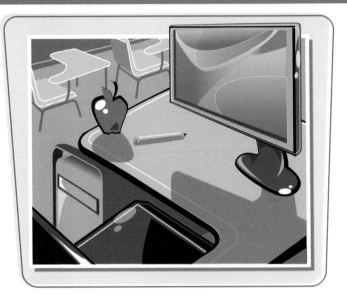

Interact with the Computer

The Mac OS is the part of the computer responsible for reading the information that you send to it by pressing keys on the keyboard, clicking the mouse, or using the trackpad. You can customize the settings for the keyboard and mouse in System Preferences.

The Finder

The Finder is an application that is always running. It displays the Desktop and windows where you can work with files, folders, and disks.

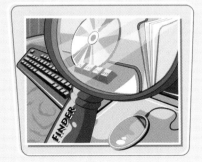

Run Applications

You can use the Mac OS to run applications. Applications are tools on your computer that help you perform particular tasks. A word processing application helps you create text-based documents. A painting application helps you to create images. An email application permits you to send and receive email.

Surf the Internet

The Mac OS provides you with everything you need to surf the World Wide Web. You can locate information with search engines, read articles, communicate with people from around the world, watch movies, do research, or even play games. The Safari Web browser gives you the means to view Web pages. Mail gives you access to the world of email.

Listen to and View Media

The Mac OS gives you a complete toolbox to use with multimedia files. You can listen to music in iTunes, catalog and view photos in iPhoto, create your own movies in iMovie, build and burn DVDs in iDVD, and even create your own music in GarageBand.

Share Files and Hardware with Others

The Mac OS helps you connect to computers anywhere on a local network or the Internet. You can share information and hardware on a network. You can share files with others or print using the same printer.

Interface with Other Equipment

The Mac OS is proficient at working with a variety of computer hardware. From a keyboard, mouse, and joystick to the iPod, video cameras, and cell phones, the Mac OS gives you the opportunity to connect your equipment to and interact with the digital hub. Your Mac can talk to all of these types of equipment and more.

Although it has only one button, a Mac mouse or trackpad can perform many different functions. You can click the mouse once or twice to achieve different results. Click once to select a file or folder for use with any Finder menu. Double-click a file or folder to select and open it. You can also modify a mouse click by pressing the `Control` key. This usually causes a contextual menu to appear.

Click the Mouse Once or Twice

SINGLE-CLICK

① Click the **Finder** icon in the Dock.

A Finder window opens if one is not already open.

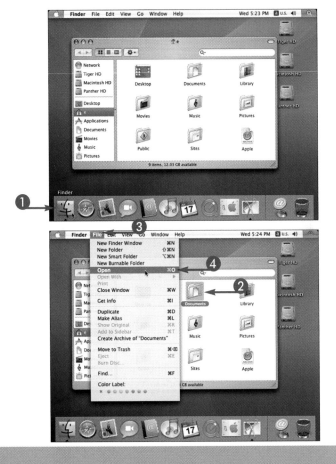

② Click a folder to select it.

The icon darkens to indicate that you have selected it.

③ Click **File**.

④ Click **Open**.

The folder opens, revealing its contents.

DOUBLE-CLICK

1 In the Finder, double-click a folder icon.

The folder opens immediately.

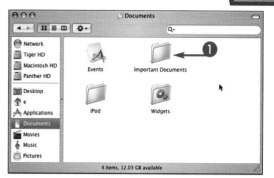

CLICK WITH A MODIFIER

1 Press Control and click once on the Finder Desktop.

A contextual menu opens revealing different functions applicable to the Desktop.

TIPS

Are there any single-click shortcuts I can use?

You can rename a file or folder by clicking its name in the Finder. After a brief pause, the name appears highlighted and waits for you to type a new name. When you finish typing the name, press Return to complete the change. If you press Return a second time, you can edit the file name again just as if you had single-clicked it. If you press ⌘, you can click multiple files in the Finder to select them. This helps when you want to perform an action on multiple items at once.

What double-click shortcuts will help me?

Press ⌘ when you double-click a folder to open the folder in a new Finder window. Press Option and double-click a folder to open it in a new window and to close the previous window.

Control the Mac with Menus

One of the main tools in the Mac OS interface is the menu. Apple designed the Mac interface with continuity in mind. You can click and use menus in any application and expect to see similar results. Menus also have similar keyboard shortcuts to trigger their actions in many applications. This helps you maintain a sense of cohesion as you work with different applications. Sometimes menus contain hidden functions that you can reveal by pressing a special modifier key.

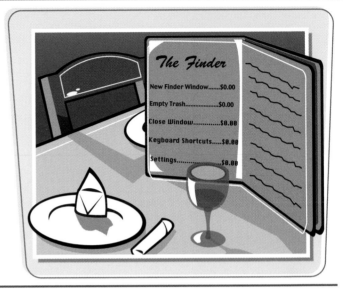

Control the Mac with Menus

CLICK A MENU

1 In the Finder, click **Go**.

2 Click **Home**.

A window opens, displaying the contents of your Home folder.

SELECT MENU ITEMS WITH THE KEYBOARD

① In the Finder, press ⌘ + Shift + U .

A window opens listing the contents of the Utilities folder.

USE HIDDEN MENU CHOICES

① Click **File**.

② Press Option .

● The appearance of the **File** menu changes and reveals hidden functions.

③ Release Option with the menu still open.

The standard **File** menu items reappear.

TIPS

Where do I find keyboard shortcuts for menus?

Keyboard shortcuts for all menu items appear in the menus themselves. A menu item displays its shortcut to the right of its title. For example, in the Finder you can open a new window by pressing ⌘ + N . The keyboard shortcut appears as the first item in the File menu with symbols for ⌘ and N .

Are there any keys that produce hidden functions in the Finder menus?

You can also press Option and Shift to reveal hidden menu functions. Hidden menu items appear in place of the usual menu items when you press either the Option or Shift key modifiers. The keyboard shortcut icons in the menu also change to reflect the keys in the keystroke.

Work with Finder Windows

Along with menus, windows are among the most important parts of the Mac OS interface. Finder windows are containers for organizing your files. You can customize windows to match your needs precisely. You can resize a window to reveal something behind it or to see more files in it. If a window gets in the way, you can minimize it, which tucks the window nicely away in the Dock for one click access later. Finally, when you are finished using a window, one simple click closes it.

Work with Finder Windows

OPEN A NEW WINDOW

① In the Finder, click **File**.

② Click **New Finder Window**.

A new Finder window opens.

RESIZE A FINDER WINDOW

① Click and drag the bottom-right corner of the window.

The window resizes as you drag.

② Click the **Zoom** button ().

The window zooms to full size.

③ Click (◯) again.

The window returns to its original size.

CLOSE A FINDER WINDOW

1 In an open Finder window, click the **Close** button ().

The Finder window closes.

MINIMIZE A FINDER WINDOW

1 In an open Finder window, click the **Minimize** button ().

The window minimizes, appearing in the dock.

2 Click the icon in the Dock.

The window returns to normal size.

Are there any shortcuts that I can use with windows?

If you press and hold Option while clicking the close button in a Finder window, all open Finder windows will close. You can cycle through the open windows of most applications by pressing ⌘ + ⌃ repeatedly. Press ⌘ + Shift + ⌃ to cycle through the open windows in reverse order. Pressing the ⌘ + M keyboard shortcut causes the foremost window to minimize in the Dock.

Why do I need to resize windows?

When you make a window larger, you can view more of the files within that window. When you make a window smaller, you see less of the files and the size of the scrollbar changes relative to how much of the window contents you cannot see. Making a window smaller also helps you to see more of other windows or the desktop behind it.

You are not restricted to viewing Finder windows in one format. You can customize the look and feel of your Finder windows to help you work more efficiently. You can change the size of icons and text in Finder windows to suit your needs. The Finder gives you several different choices for displaying information about files. You can customize these choices to change the amount of information that appears in a window.

Change Window View Options

OPEN VIEW OPTIONS

① In the Finder, click **View**.

② Click **Show view Options**.

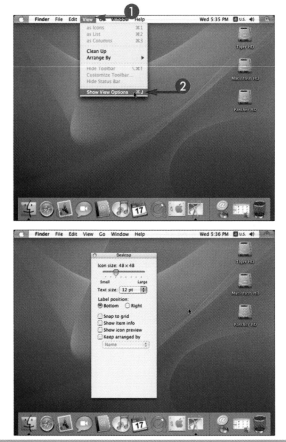

The View Options window opens, displaying settings for the foremost window. If no window is open, the settings for the Desktop appear in the View Options window instead.

ARRANGE ICONS AUTOMATICALLY

① In the View Options window, click **Keep Arranged By** (☐ changes to ☑).

Make sure that the window is in Icon or List view, or you will not see these settings.

② Click ⬚ and select **Kind**.

The icons in the window automatically sort themselves according to file type. The Finder maintains this automatic sorting even when you resize a window or add and remove files.

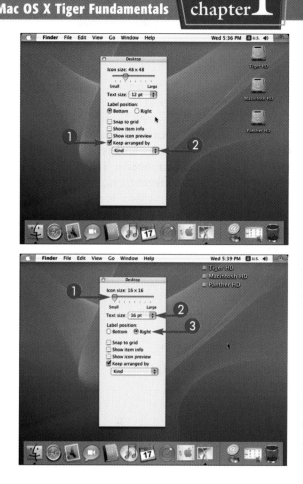

CHANGE ICON AND TEXT SIZE

① In the View Options window, drag ⬚ left to **16x16**.

The icons appear at 16x16, the smallest size. Make certain that the window is in Icon or List view, or you will not see these settings.

② Click ⬚ and select **16 pt**.

③ Click **Right** (◯ changes to ●).

The Finder updates the window to reflect the changes.

TIPS

What does the Show Icon Preview option in the View Options window do?

For graphics files like JPG, TIF, and PNG, the Finder displays a preview of the image as an icon for each file. That way, you can tell what the image contains without opening the file to see. You merely glance at its preview icon. Note that this only works for the Icon and List views.

Can I change the white background of my Finder windows?

You can set the background of Finder windows using the settings that appear at the bottom of the View Options window. Click **Color** to select a color for the background. Click **Picture** to choose a picture file to use as the window background. If you click **All Windows**, the window background color or image appears on any Icon view windows that you open thereafter.

Understanding Applications

Applications are the main workhorses of the Mac OS. They are functional units that help you perform tasks with the computer. Some applications play music, some display images, and others create documents or even play games. You can launch an application either by clicking its icon in the Dock or double-clicking its icon in the Finder.

Understanding Applications

OPEN THE APPLICATIONS FOLDER

① In the Finder, press ⌘ + Shift + A.

The Applications window opens, showing all applications installed in the Applications folder.

LAUNCH AN APPLICATION

① In the Applications folder, double-click **TextEdit**.

The TextEdit application launches and opens a new document where you can type text.

② Click the **Safari** icon.

The Safari Web browser launches.

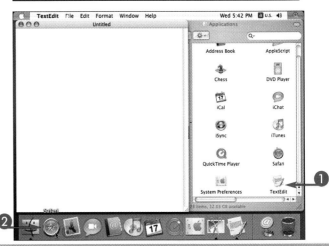

QUIT AN APPLICATION

① From any running application, click the application menu.

② Click **Quit**.

The application stops.

LOCATE RUNNING APPLICATIONS

① In the Dock, locate the small black triangles that appear beneath running applications.

② Click an icon of a running application.

The application comes to the foreground.

What kinds of things can I do with the applications that come installed with Mac OS and iLife?

You can perform a wide variety of tasks with the applications that accompany OS X. You can listen to, catalog, and record music. You can organize, edit, and share photos, create word processing documents, keep track of addresses, email friends, surf the Internet, watch and create movies, make calendars, and play chess.

Are there other applications available to me in case the applications in OS X do not provide what I need?

You can download literally thousands of applications on the Internet, many of which are free or available for a small fee. There are applications to perform almost any task imaginable. With applications, you can track your music and book collection, play a game of golf, draw a picture, balance your checkbook, or even learn to juggle. Two of the most popular software download sites are www.versiontracker.com and www.macupdate.com.

The Dock is a one-stop utility that performs different tasks. You can launch applications from the Dock, see which applications are running, and give yourself one-click access to commonly used files. You can quit applications by clicking icons in the Dock. You can also add folders to the Dock, so you can access all of its contents with a single click.

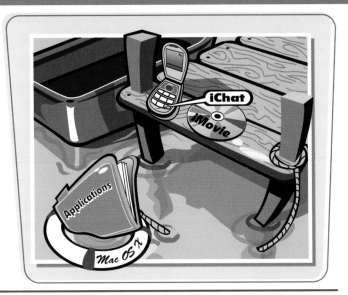

Using the Dock

LAUNCH AN APPLICATION FROM THE DOCK

① In the Dock, click **Safari**.

The Safari Web browser launches.

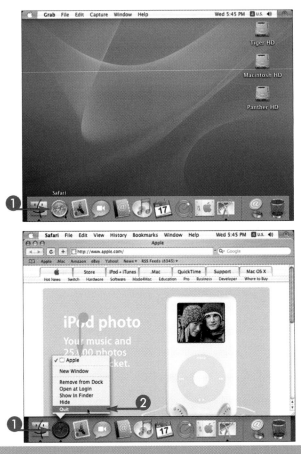

QUIT AN APPLICATION FROM THE DOCK

① In the Dock, click the icon of a running application and continue holding the mouse button.

● A pop-up menu lists functions for the application.

② Click **Quit**.

The application stops.

ADD A FOLDER TO THE DOCK

① In the Finder, press `Control` + `Shift` + `H` to open your Home folder.

② Click and drag the **Pictures** folder from the Home folder to a position on the Dock.

An icon appears in the Dock.

③ Click the **Pictures** folder icon in the Dock to open the **Pictures** folder.

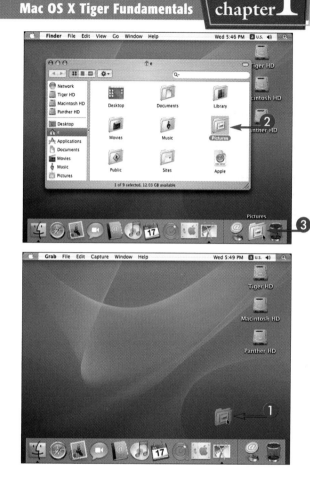

REMOVE A FILE FROM THE DOCK

① Click and drag an application, document, or file icon from the Dock to the Desktop.

The icon disappears from the Dock in an animated puff of smoke.

TIPS

If I remove an icon from the Dock, does it erase that item from the hard drive?

No. The elements in the Dock are simply pointers to applications, files, or folders that those icons represent. Removing the icons from the Dock does nothing more than remove the icon from the Dock. It does not affect any application, file, or folder.

Why is there a vertical line on the Dock?

The vertical line in the Dock separates applications from the files and folders that you place in the Dock.

Toggle Applications

You can switch between all running applications with one keystroke. The Application Switcher takes care of switching applications when you press the keystroke. You can also control the Application Switcher with the keyboard to make switching even easier.

SWITCH TO ANOTHER APPLICATION

① Press ⌘ + Tab.

The Application Switcher displays all running applications.

② While holding down ⌘, press Tab again.

● The Application Switcher highlights the next icon in the list.

③ When the application you want to launch is highlighted, release ⌘.

The highlighted application comes to the foreground.

④ While holding down ⌘ + Shift, press Tab.

The Application Switcher highlights the previous icon.

SWITCH APPLICATIONS WITH ARROW KEYS

① Press ⌘ + Tab.

The Application Switcher appears, displaying icons of all running applications.

② While holding down ⌘, press →.

● The Application Switcher highlights the next icon in the list.

③ While holding ⌘, press ←.

The Application Switcher highlights the previous icon in the list.

④ When the icon for the application you want to launch is highlighted, release ⌘.

The highlighted application comes to the foreground.

Mac OS is a multiuser operating system, which means that more than one user can use the same computer with personalized settings that each user determines and controls. To use the computer, you must login using your user name and password. Logging in can prevent other users from changing your settings or using your account.

Logging In and Out

LOG OUT

1 Click the **Apple** icon (🍎).

2 Click **Log Out Username**.

A window appears asking you to confirm your logout operation.

3 Click the **Logout** button.

Your account logs out and displays the Login dialog box.

LOG IN

1 Click a user icon.

2 Type your password into the password field that appears.

3 Click **Login**.

The computer logs you in.

You can put your computer to sleep instead of shutting it down. A sleeping Mac uses very little energy and has the benefit of allowing instant-on access to your computer. These features are especially useful for laptops, which rely on battery power that you need to conserve.

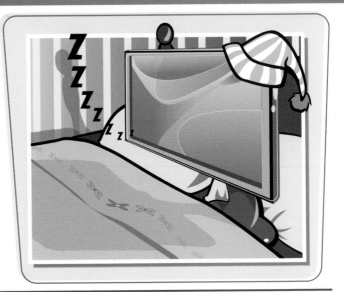

Put Your Mac to Sleep

MAKE THE MAC GO TO SLEEP

1 Click 🍎.

2 Click **Sleep**.

The Mac goes to sleep and displays nothing on the screen.

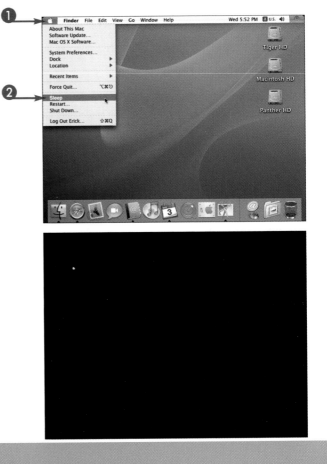

3 Press any key, or click the mouse or trackpad.

The computer awakens instantly, permitting you to pick up where you left off when you put the computer to sleep.

MAKE A LAPTOP SLEEP

1 To put an iBook or PowerBook to sleep, simply close the laptop lid.

The computer goes to sleep, and on some models a pulsating light appears on the outside cover indicating sleep.

2 Open the laptop, and press any key or click the trackpad.

The computer awakens to where you last worked.

TIPS

What happens when a Mac is in sleep mode?

When you put a Mac to sleep, it disables the network settings and puts the computer in a low-power mode. It will remember unsaved documents that you were working on, but it will not permit file sharing on the network.

Do I have to worry about the battery running out while sleeping?

Although the computer uses a low-power mode during sleep, it is still using battery power that can cause the battery to drain. When a laptop battery gets below a certain level of remaining power, the Mac shuts off automatically, which means that you could lose unsaved data.

Restart or Shut Down the Mac

Although a Macintosh can run nonstop for days and weeks on end, there are times when you may need to shut down or restart a Mac. It is useful to shut down a computer when you need to move the machine, when there is an electrical storm, or when you want to install new hardware. Restarting a Mac is required after some software installations and also sometimes helps fix an errant machine.

Restart or Shut Down the Mac

RESTART A MAC

① Click the **Apple** icon.

② Click **Restart**.

A dialog box appears asking you to approve the restart.

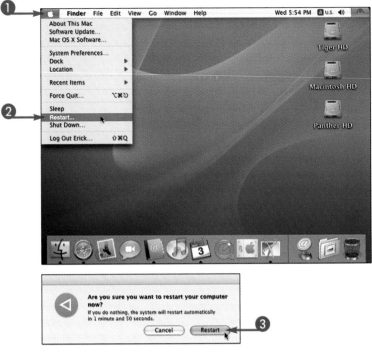

③ Click **Restart**.

The computer restarts.

SHUT DOWN

1 Click .

2 Click **Shut Down**.

A dialog box asks you to approve the shutdown process.

3 Click **Shut Down**.

The computer shuts down.

What happens when my computer restarts?

If you have the default single-user settings in the Users pane of the System Preferences, your computer restarts and your Desktop appears. If you use a computer in a multiuser environment, you may have to provide a login username and password when you restart the computer.

When should I shut down a computer instead of put it to sleep?

You should shut down a Mac before physically moving it or disconnecting its power source. It is also probably a good idea to shut down and disconnect the power to a computer during an electrical storm. If you do not plan on doing any of the aforementioned tasks, you can safely use the sleep function instead.

Get Help

If you get stuck while using your Mac, you can sometimes get out of a jam by consulting the Finder's built-in Help system. The Help system contains valuable information about using both hardware and software related to the Mac.

Get Help

LAUNCH HELP FOR THE FINDER

① In the Finder, click **Help**.

② Click **Mac Help**.

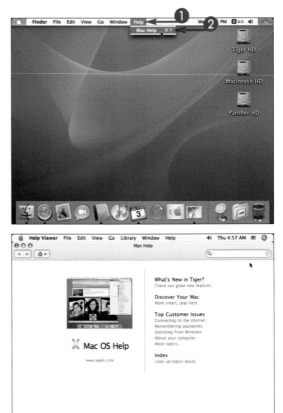

The Help Viewer launches and displays helpful information about the Finder.

FIND ANSWERS

① In the Help Viewer, type a question into the **Search** field.

② Press Return.

The Help Viewer finds answers to your question and displays the results.

TIPS

I know how to use the Finder. Can I locate help for other applications too?

The Help menu in all applications is context-specific. When you click **Help**, the Help Viewer application displays information specific to the current application.

Is the Help system limited to information for Apple applications only?

The Help menu can display useful information for any application that includes built-in Help. You can search any installed Help modules just as you would search the one for the Finder.

2

Mastering the Finder

Are you ready to locate files more quickly than ever? This chapter shows you how to use Tiger's new, powerful search tools. You also learn to customize the Finder so it fits the way you work.

Find the
Home Folder

Mac OS X is a multiuser operating system. In a multiuser operating system, each user is allocated space on the hard drive for personal files and preferences. This space is called the Home folder. You can put all of your files safely into your Home folder without worrying that an unauthorized user will alter or erase them.

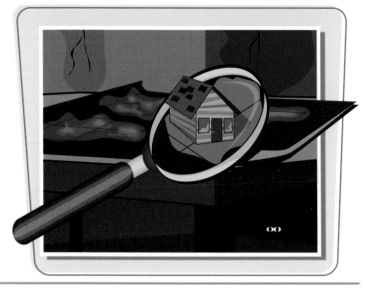

LOCATE HOME

① In the Finder, click **Go**.

② Click **Home**.

The house icon (🏠) lets you know you are viewing your own Home folder.

A window displays the current user's Home folder.

③ While holding down ⌘, click the title bar of the window.

A pop-up menu opens, showing you the actual location of the current Home folder.

④ Click **Users**.

The Users folder appears.

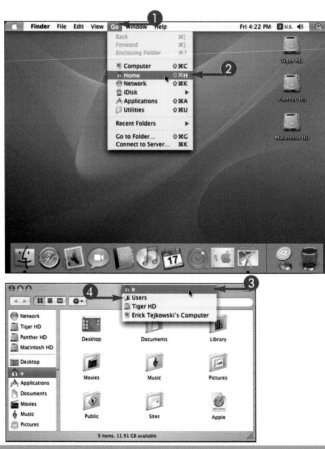

The Users folder contains the Home folder of every user on a computer; the current user's Home folder retains the 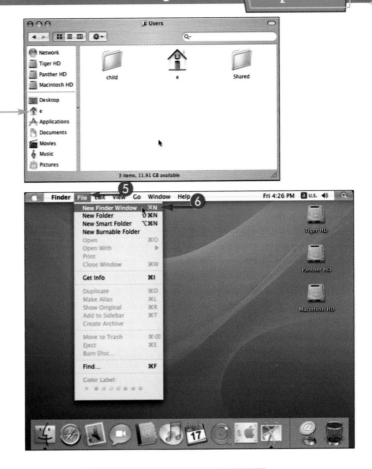, while all other Home folders display a ⬜.

● You can also click 🏠 to open the Home folder.

⑤ Click **File**.

⑥ Click **New Finder Window**.

A new Finder window opens, displaying the current Home folder.

TIP

Can a new Finder window open by default to another location besides the Home folder?

Yes. Although new Finder windows open to the Home folder when you first install Mac OS X Tiger, you can change the default location. Open the Finder Preferences located in the Finder menu to adjust the setting. You will find it in the **General** section of the Finder preferences window. You can select the Desktop, a hard drive, or any other folder on your system as the default location for new Finder windows.

Save Time Using Contextual Menus

To save yourself frequent trips to the menu bar at the top of the screen, make use of contextual menus. Using contextual menus reduces the number of repetitive wrist actions, and the menus are usually more quickly accessible than standard menus. For example, you can change the Desktop background in two clicks using a contextual menu. The same procedure without a contextual menu would require twice as many clicks.

Save Time Using Contextual Menus

SET THE DESKTOP BACKGROUND

① While holding down Control, click the Desktop.

A contextual menu lists functions appropriate to the Desktop.

② Click **Change Desktop Background**.

The System Preferences window opens with the Desktop & Screen Saver pane active.

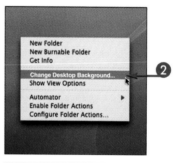

③ Select an image for the desktop.

The Desktop background changes.

④ Click 🔴.

CREATE A FOLDER

1. While holding down `Control`, click the Desktop.

2. Click **New Folder**.

   A new folder appears on the Desktop, named untitled folder.

MOVE A FOLDER TO THE TRASH

1. While holding down `Control`, click a folder.

   A contextual menu appears.

2. Click **Move To Trash**.

   The folder disappears into the Trash.

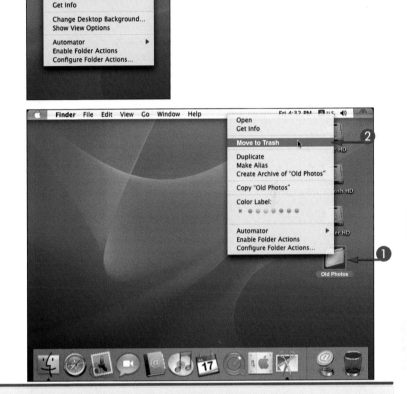

TIPS

Can I use contextual menus in other applications?

Each application uses contextual menus differently. Try Control-clicking various places in an application to see if it supports contextual menus. For example, a Safari web page displays functions in its contextual menu for saving and printing that page. Likewise, iTunes displays contextual menu item functions that pertain to songs and playlists depending on which one you Control-click.

What kinds of functions can I add to Finder contextual menus and how do I install them?

You can download contextual menu plug-ins freely from the Internet. Some plug-ins help you perform Finder tasks more quickly. Other plug-ins act as miniature multimedia applications, playing video and audio file previews. Install any third-party contextual menu plug-ins that you download by placing them in ~/Library/Contextual Menu Items, where ~ represents your Home folder.

Increase Productivity with the Sidebar

With the Sidebar feature of Finder windows, you have instant access to common locations on your hard drive and servers like iDisk. You can also use the Sidebar as a launcher for one-click access to your favorite applications and files.

ADD AN ALIAS TO THE SIDEBAR

1. In the Finder, click **File**.

2. Click **New Finder Window**.

   A Finder window opens.

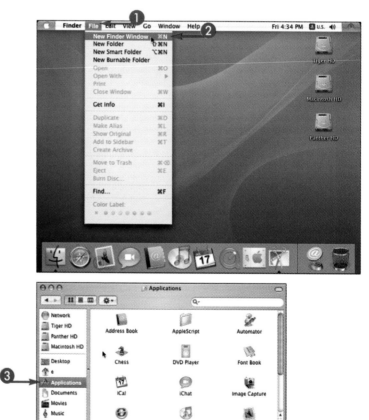

3. Click **Applications**.

   The Finder window displays the contents of the Applications folder.

32

④ Click and drag an application into the Sidebar.

● An alias to the application appears in the Sidebar.

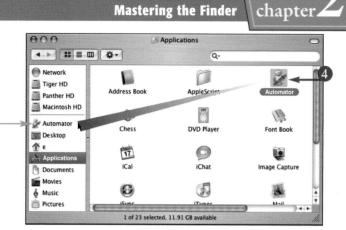

DELETE AN ALIAS FROM THE SIDEBAR

① Click and drag an application icon from the Sidebar to anywhere outside the Sidebar.

When you release the mouse button, the icon no longer appears in Finder windows.

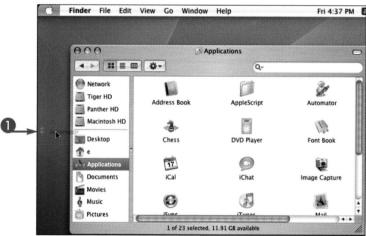

TIP

How can I remove the Sidebar from my Finder windows?

There are four ways that you can remove the Sidebar from Finder windows. First, click the button in the top-right corner of each Finder window. Doing this causes the Sidebar and Toolbar to toggle on and off. Likewise, you can toggle the display of these elements using Hide/Show Toolbar in the View menu of the Finder. Lastly, you can also hide the Sidebar by clicking and dragging its right edge leftwards, making it so small that the Sidebar disappears. You can also double-click the dividing line to toggle it open and closed. If you mistakenly remove an item from the Sidebar, simply drag a new copy of the file or folder to the Sidebar of any open window. A new icon appears in place of the old one.

Organize Your Windows

While working with various applications, your work environment can easily become cluttered, making it difficult to find things. Tiger helps with this problem by giving you an important feature called Exposé. Exposé is a hidden window manager that springs into action with only one keystroke. You can use Exposé to quickly organize your desktop.

SELECT A WINDOW IN THE FINDER

① In the Finder, open several Finder windows.

Note: To open a Finder window, see Chapter 1.

Open as many windows as you want; more open windows results in a more impressive display.

② Press F10.

All open Finder windows instantly tile so that you can see each one.

③ Move the mouse around the Desktop.

Each window highlights and displays its name as you move the mouse over it.

④ Click a window with which you want to work.

The windows return to normal size with the selected window in the foreground.

⑤ If you decide to not work with a window, press F10 again.

TIPS

Does this feature work with all application windows?

Pressing F10 causes the windows of only the foremost application to collapse. The foremost application displays its title at the top of the application menu. It is also the application with which you are currently working and whose name appears in the top left corner of your screen.

How can I slow down the Exposé animation?

Before pressing F9, F10, or F11, press and hold Shift. When you activate any of the Exposé functions, the animation will move in slow motion. This "feature" doesn't really have a function other than to look neat.

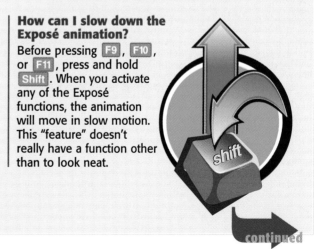

continued

In addition to cleaning up the windows for a specific application, Exposé can organize windows of all open applications for easy access. You can also cause all windows to slide instantaneously from the screen, revealing the Desktop hiding beneath them. This gives you immediate access to the files and disks on the Desktop.

Organize Your Windows *(continued)*

SELECT A WINDOW FROM RUNNING APPLICATIONS

1 Launch two or three more applications and open a couple windows in each.

You can launch any applications you want, so long as they each have at least one open window.

2 Press F9.

All open windows instantly resize and reposition so that you can see each one.

3 Move the mouse around the Desktop.

Each window highlights and displays its name as you move the mouse over it.

④ Click the window with which you want to work.

The windows return to normal size with the selected window in the foreground.

If you decide to not work with a window, you can press F9 again.

The windows return to normal size.

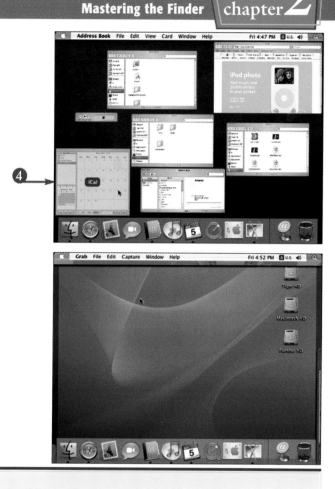

UNCOVER THE DESKTOP

① Press F11.

All windows immediately slide off the screen, revealing the Desktop.

② Press F11 again.

All windows immediately slide back into their original positions, obscuring the Desktop again.

TIPS

Can I use Exposé with fewer keystrokes?

The F9, F10, and F11 keys can behave as both a toggle and a momentary switch. To toggle, press the key and let go. Then, press the key to return the previous state. To use Exposé functions as a momentary switch, press and hold the appropriate key. Then, let go of the key to return to the previous state.

Does drag and drop work between Exposé windows?

You can drag and drop files between two windows. For example, to drag a file from the Desktop to another window, show the Desktop by pressing and holding F11. Click a file on the Desktop and begin to drag it, but do not let go of the mouse button. Release F11 and press F9 to reveal all open windows of the foremost applications. Drag the mouse over the destination window. When it opens, let go of the mouse to complete the drag-and-drop operation.

Customize Icons

Mac OS X Tiger displays beautiful icons, but sometimes you want to customize the interface with icons you find on the Internet. You can change the icon of any file or folder with just a few mouse clicks.

Customizing icons does more than spruce up a lackluster Finder window. You can use icons to visually organize folders for different purposes. Icons also help you work faster, since you can recognize familiar icons quicker than reading a file's name.

Customize Icons

CHANGE A FILE'S ICON

① In the Finder, click a file that displays the icon you want to use.

② Click **Edit**.

③ Click **Copy**.

A reference to the file is copied to the Clipboard.

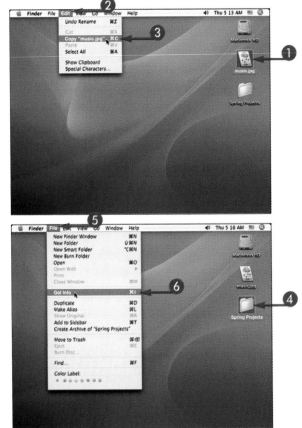

④ Click a file or folder whose icon you want to change.

⑤ Click **File**.

⑥ Click **Get Info**.

The Info window for the destination file opens.

⑦ Click the icon in the Info window to select it.

The icon highlights to show that you selected it.

⑧ Click **Edit**.

⑨ Click **Paste**.

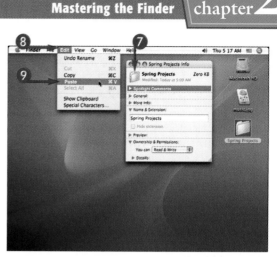

● The icon of the destination file changes to match the original icon.

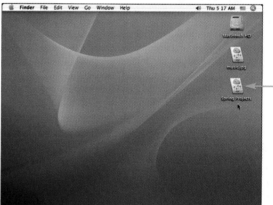

Where can I find icons to use in the Finder?

The Internet is loaded with all sorts of free icons for you to use in Tiger. One of the premiere icon sites for Mac OS is The Icon factory at www.iconfactory.com, where you can find hundreds of free icons to download. The popular website, ResExcellence, also hosts a significant Mac OS free icon collection at http://resexcellence.com/.

Can I change the icons of all files and folders?

You can change the icon of many files and folders in the Finder, with some exceptions. You may only change the icon for a file or folder if you have write access for it. You can find **Ownership and Permissions** in the same **Get Info** window where you paste the icon onto the file or folder. The **Ownership and Permissions** section of the Get Info window will tell you if you are permitted to write to that file or folder. If you are permitted, then you can change its icon.

Duplicate Files

Knowing how to make a copy of a file or folder is an important task. Sometimes you may want to work on a copy of a file, so that you do not alter the original. Other times, you may want to make a backup of a file for safekeeping. You can duplicate files in the Finder in one of four ways: with a menu, by using a keyboard shortcut, with copy and paste, and via drag and drop.

Duplicate Files

COPY A FILE WITH A MENU

1. In the Finder, click a file that you want to duplicate.
2. Click **File**.
3. Click **Duplicate**.

   The Finder makes a copy of the file.

BACK UP A FILE WITH A KEYBOARD SHORTCUT

1. In the Finder, click a file to back up.
2. Press ⌘ + D.
   - The Finder makes a copy of the file.

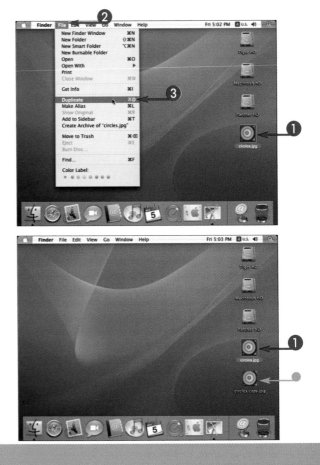

CLONE A FILE WITH COPY AND PASTE

① In the Finder, click a file that you would like to duplicate.

② Press ⌘+C.

③ Navigate to the folder in which you want the duplicate file to appear.

④ Click **Edit.**

⑤ Click **Paste.**

The Finder makes a copy of the file in the destination folder.

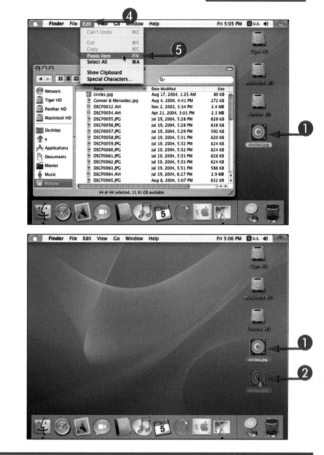

REPLICATE FILES WITH DRAG AND DROP

① On the Desktop, click a file that you want to duplicate.

② While pressing Option , click and drag the file to where you want the duplicate to appear.

The Finder makes a copy of the file in the destination.

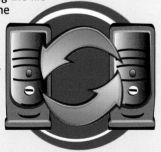

TIPS

What steps do I need to take to copy a file from one hard drive to another disk?

Copying a file from one disk to another is easy. Simply click and drag the file from the source disk to the destination disk. The Finder assumes that you want to make a copy. No other tasks are necessary. If you drag a file from one location to another location on the same disk, the Finder simply moves the file to the destination folder.

I copied the wrong file. Now what should I do?

Before doing anything else, press ⌘+Z to undo the copy operation. Then, proceed with the desired copy operation. You can only undo one Finder command at a time, so make sure that you undo the operation immediately if you want it to take effect. Of course, you can also simply delete any files that you may have inadvertently copied by dragging them to the Trash.

Delete Files

Not every file is worth keeping, so you need the ability to delete a file. You can delete a file in one of three ways: using a Finder menu, pressing a keyboard shortcut, and clicking a contextual menu.

DELETE A FILE

1. In the Finder, click a file that you want to delete.
2. Click **File**.
3. Click **Move to Trash**.

   The Finder moves the file to the Trash.

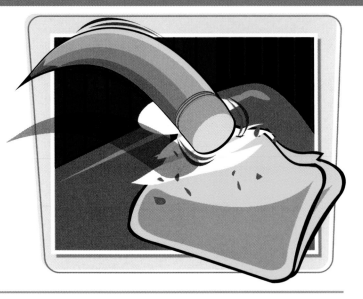

MOVE A FILE TO THE TRASH USING THE KEYBOARD

1. In the Finder, click the file you want to delete.
2. Press ⌘ + Delete.

   The Finder moves the file to the Trash.

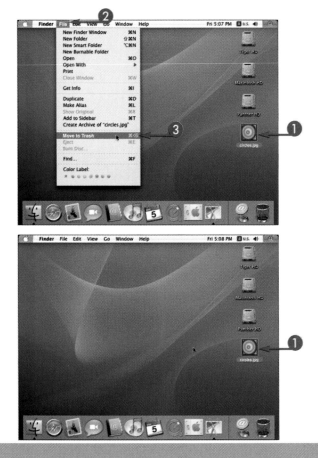

REMOVE A FILE WITH A CONTEXTUAL MENU

① In the Finder, press and hold Control.

② Click a file to delete.

● A contextual menu appears.

③ Click **Move to Trash**.

The Finder moves the file to the Trash.

EMPTY THE TRASH

① Click **Finder**.

② Click **Empty Trash**.

The Finder permanently removes files from the Trash.

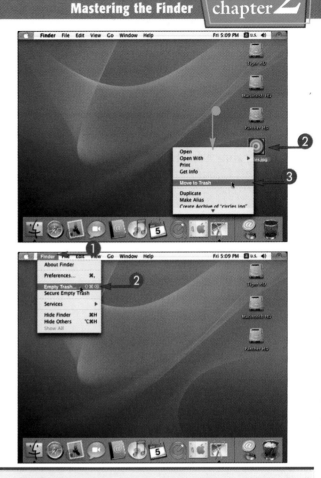

TIPS

I moved a file to the Trash, but want to use it again. What should I do?

So long as the file is still in the Trash, you can retrieve it and drag it to some other location in the Finder. Once you empty the Trash, however, the file is gone and difficult to retrieve without third-party software.

What is the difference between Empty Trash and Secure Empty Trash in the Finder menu?

When the Finder empties the Trash, it does not erase the files. Instead it marks the places on your disk where those files resided as safe to erase in the future when the Mac OS requires more disk space. Secure Empty Trash, on the other hand, really does "erase" the file completely by writing over the location on the disk multiple times with random data. This ensures that your data is beyond recovery.

Work Quickly with Keyboard Shortcuts

The Mac OS is famous for its menus, but there is no reason you have to be tied to them. You can perform many Finder functions with the keyboard. Each menu item lists its keyboard shortcut next to its title. Some keyboard shortcuts require special keys. The Command key is represented by ⌘. The Option key is represented by Option. The Shift key is represented by Shift and the Control key by Control.

Work Quickly with Keyboard Shortcuts

USE COMMON KEYBOARD SHORTCUTS

① In the Finder, click **Finder**.

The File menu opens, displaying the functions in that menu.

② Press ⌘ + Shift + Delete.

The Finder asks you if you really want to permanently empty the Trash.

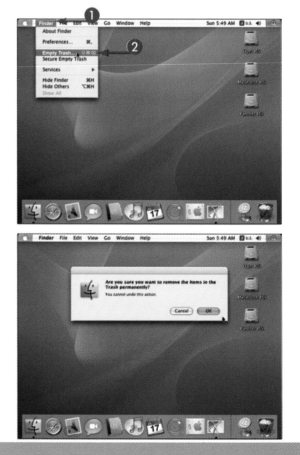

③ Press Enter or Return.

Pressing Esc activates the Cancel button on-screen.

USE HIDDEN KEYBOARD SHORTCUTS

1 In the Finder, click **File.**

2 Press and hold Option .

The Open With, Close Window, and Get Info menus change to Always Open With, Close All, and Show Inspector, respectively.

3 Release Option to revert the menu items to their original functionality.

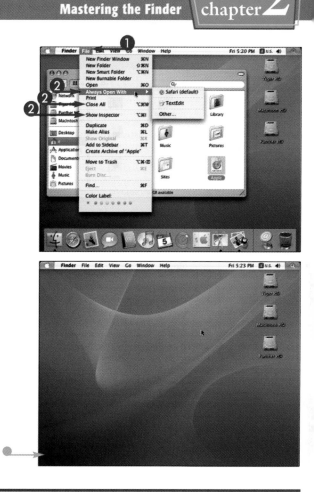

SHOW AND HIDE THE DOCK

1 Press ⌘ + Option + D .

● The Dock disappears from view.

2 Press ⌘ + Option + D .

The Dock returns to its previous position.

TIPS

Are there any other keyboard shortcuts I should know about?

Whenever the Finder asks you to approve or cancel an operation, it displays a dialog box that contains an OK button and a Cancel button. You can press Return or Enter to mimic clicking OK button. Press Esc to cancel the operation.

How can I restart or shut down my computer without using the mouse?

Press Control + ⏏ to open the Shutdown window. In this window, you can restart the computer by pressing R , put the computer to sleep by pressing S , shut down the computer by pressing Return or Esc to cancel the operation and close the window.

Get Info about Files

The Finder normally displays some basic information about a file in List View, but there is much more to know about a file. You can locate detailed information about a file in the Info window. The Info window (sometimes also called the Get Info window) displays important information like file size, creation and modification dates, file type, and permissions.

Get Info about Files

1. In the Finder, click a file that you would like to know more about.

2. Click **File**.

3. Click **Get Info.**

   The Info window opens, displaying additional information about that file.

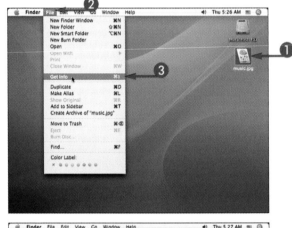

4. Click the disclosure triangles at the left edge of the window to reveal different categories of information about a file.

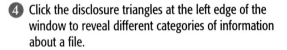

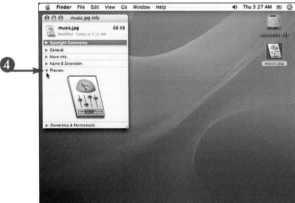

5 Click to expand the **Name & Extension** section.

The Info displays the file's name and a checkbox for toggling the file extension. When the Hide extension option is selected, the Finder will not display the period and two or more characters at the end of a filename.

6 Change the name of the file and press Return .

7 Click ⊗ .

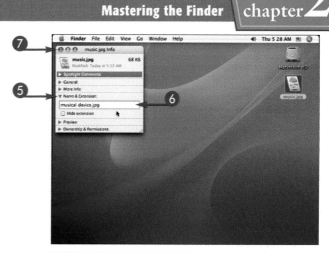

● The Finder renames the file based on what you typed in the Info window.

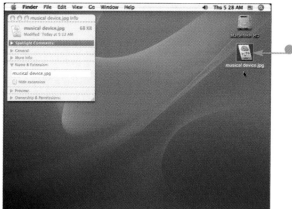

What do all of those other sections in the Info window do?

Section	What it displays
General	Kind, Size, Location, and Creation/Modification Dates.
Name & Extension	The file's name and filename extension, which consists of a period followed by two or more alphanumeric characters.
Open with	The application that the Finder will use to open this if you double-click it.
Preview	A 128x128 copy of the file's icon or if the file is a type that QuickTime recognizes, a small preview player.
Ownership & Permissions	Who can read the file and write to it.
Spotlight Comments	Text that you enter, which Spotlight can read to learn more about a file or folder.
Plug-ins	A list of plug-ins available to certain applications.
More Info	Displays context-sensitive information about a file. For example, the dimensions of a JPEG.

Create File Archives

A file archive is a compressed and consolidated version of one or more files. A compressed file is favorable because it takes up less space. This saves room on your hard drive and makes the file move more quickly over the Internet should you decide to email it. The Finder has file archiving and extracting features. Some files do not compress when you archive them, becaues they are already in a compressed state (like JPEG). You can still benefit from the fact that a single archive file can contain multiple files.

Create File Archives

USING THE FINDER'S ARCHIVE FUNCTIONS

1. In the Finder, press and hold **Control**.
2. Click a file that you want to archive.

    A contextual menu opens.
3. Click **Create Archive of...**.

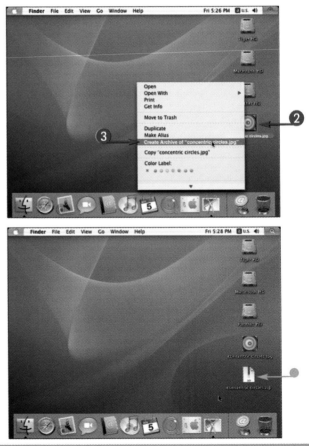

- The Finder creates an archive of the file and appends the .zip extension to the filename of the new archive.

4. Click and drag the file archive into an email to send it.

EXTRACT AN ARCHIVED FILE

① Locate a ZIP file archive whose contents you want to extract.

② Double-click the archive to convert it to an uncompressed file or group of files.

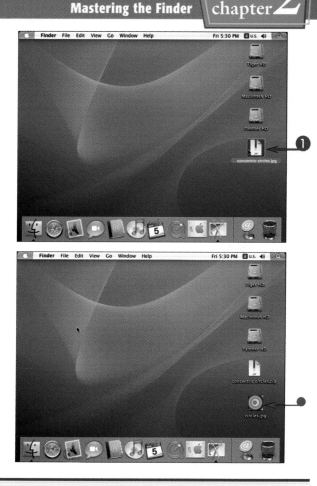

● The Finder extracts the data from the archive, restoring it to its pre-archived state.

TIPS

Can I send ZIP archives to friends who use Microsoft Windows?

The ZIP format is a universally understood archive format. Microsoft Windows users can extract them, as can Linux, Unix, and other Mac users. There are other archive formats, but ZIP is probably the most universal now.

How much space can I conserve by archiving a file?

Although space savings can vary among files, it is not uncommon to reduce a 30MB file that contains textual data to only 3MB by archiving it, a 90-percent reduction. A file one-tenth its original size requires only one-tenth of the time to send over email or to download from a Web page. Some file formats, like TIFF, compress well while others, such as MP3 and JPEG, cannot be compressed, as they are already compressed formats. You can only compress a file once.

3

Customizing Tiger with the System Preferences

The System Preferences is the main control center of Mac OS X Tiger. In the System Preferences window, you can adjust a variety of settings, such as the Desktop appearance and the behavior of different Finder applications, to personalize your Tiger experience.

Change the Appearance of the Mac Interface

You can change the appearance of your desktop by selecting a desired color or photo as the pattern that it displays. Change the text highlight color to suit your preferences. You can also keep track of recently used application, documents, and servers.

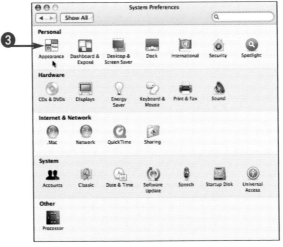

Change the Appearance of the Mac Interface

ADJUST THE DESKTOP COLOR

1 Click

2 Click **System Preferences**.

The System Preferences window opens.

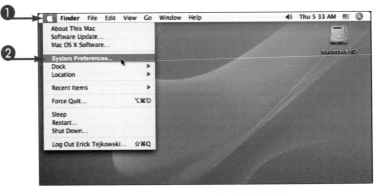

3 Click **Appearance**.

The Appearance pane of the System Preferences opens.

④ Click ⬚ and select one of the two colors.

The color scheme of the Mac OS changes.

⑤ Click ⬚ and select a highlight color.

● Tiger uses the highlight color for text selections and to show when an icon is selected in the Finder.

TIPS

What do the Number of Recent Items settings in the Appearance pane control do?

The Number of Recent Items settings in the Appearance pane of the System Preferences window control the number of items that appear in the Recent Items menu. You can find the Recent Items submenu in the Apple menu. The Recent Items menu displays the most recent applications, documents, and servers that you have used.

Why would I want to turn off text smoothing in the Appearance pane for certain font sizes ?

Mac OS X displays fonts and graphics with a large amount of "fuzziness" added. This help makes curves in letters look good. The problem is that at smaller font sizes, letters begin looking less good and more fuzzy. The Appearance pane lets you ignore font smoothing for the smallest fonts of your choosing, so you can match it to your Mac's display.

Customize Your Desktop Background

The Desktop background is something that you will look at a lot. To make it more interesting, you can add images to it, or even animate the background. You can customize your Desktop background in the Desktop pane of the System Preferences window.

SET THE DESKTOP BACKGROUND

① In System Preferences, click **Desktop & Screen Saver**.

Note: To view System Preferences, see the previous section, "Change the Appearance of the Mac Interface."

The Desktop tab of Desktop & Screen Saver pane System Preferences opens.

② Click **Apple Images**.

● When you select an image group, the preview pane displays thumbnails of the images in that group.

③ Click an image.

● The Desktop background changes.

STRETCH AND TILE THE DESKTOP BACKGROUND

1 Click **Pictures Folder**.

Thumbnails of images in your Pictures folder appear in the preview pane.

Note: The Pictures folder is located in your Home folder.

2 Click an image.

3 Click **Stretch to fill screen**.

The image resizes to cover the entire Desktop.

● Click **Tile** to fill the Desktop with multiple copies of the image at its original size.

ANIMATE THE DESKTOP BACKGROUND

1 Click **Change picture** (□ changes to ☑).

The Desktop displays the images from the currently selected group in sequence.

● Here, images from the Pictures folder are displayed.

2 Click 🔄 and select a time interval.

The Desktop background displays a different image for the chosen duration, with a smooth transition between each image.

TIPS

I cannot see the pop-up menu that allows me to enable tiled backgrounds. Where can I find it?

The pop-up menu appears only after you click **Pictures Folder**, **Choose Folder**, or any other group that contains images.

Does an animated background slow down the performance of my computer?

The animated background feature takes advantage of today's advanced video cards to provide smooth animations. If your computer does not have a high-powered video card, you may notice a slight delay when pictures change. You can decrease this delay by increasing the time between picture changes or reducing the Colors setting in the Displays pane of the System Preferences.

Play a
Screen Saver

When you are away from your computer, you can display a Screen Saver on your monitor. You can adjust the settings for Screen Savers in the System Preferences. Some Screen Savers display attractive photos on the screen while others wash the screen in colorful and mesmerizing computer animations. You can adjust the settings for some Screen Savers to alter the appearance of some or all aspects of the graphical display.

① In System Preferences, click **Desktop & Screen Saver**.

Note: To view System Preferences, see the section "Change the Appearance of the Mac Interface," earlier in this chapter.

The Desktop & Screen Saver pane of System Preferences opens.

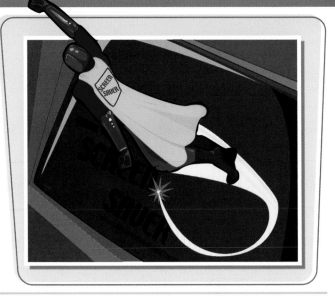

② Click **Screen Saver**.

③ Click a screen saver.

● A preview of the selected screen saver begins playing.

④ Click **Options**.

If the current selection has options to set, a menu appears displaying those options.

● Click options to select them (☐ changes to ☑).

Note: Not all screen savers offer display options.

⑤ Click **OK** to apply your changes or **Cancel** to revert to the previous settings.

The Display Options sheet closes.

⑥ Click **Test**.

The Desktop goes black and then the current Screen Saver runs in full-screen preview mode.

⑦ Click the Desktop or move the cursor to stop the Screen Saver.

You return to the System Preferences window.

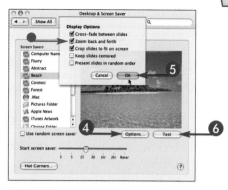

What purpose does the Pictures folder serve in the list of Screen Savers?

When you select the Pictures folder in the settings, the Screen Saver displays a slideshow of the images in your Pictures folder.

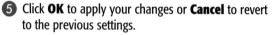

Are these the only screen savers I can use? Are there others available?

You can download many screen savers from the Internet. You can find screen savers that display interesting designs, useful information, and even live video from your own Web, iSight, or DV camera. Some screen savers scan scientific data in search of alien life forms and others display QuickTime movies. Try searching www.Google.com for OS X Screen Savers. You may be surprised at the large selection available to you.

Tweak the Dock

The Dock is a centerpiece of the OS X interface. It serves as a launcher and displays running applications, folders, and currently open files. You can customize the size of the Dock, as well as where you want the Dock to appear on your desktop. You can adjust the Dock settings in System Preferences.

Tweak the Dock

① In System Preferences, click **Dock**.

Note: To view System Preferences, see the section "Change the Appearance of the Mac Interface."

The Dock settings appear.

CHANGE THE DOCK SIZE

② Click and drag the Dock Size slider (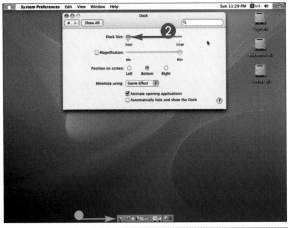) to **Small**.

● The dock icons decrease in size.

CHANGE THE DOCK MAGNIFICATION

③ Click **Magnification** (☐ changes to ☑).

④ Click and drag 🔘 to **Max**.

● The Dock icons momentarily increase in size as you move a mouse over the Dock.

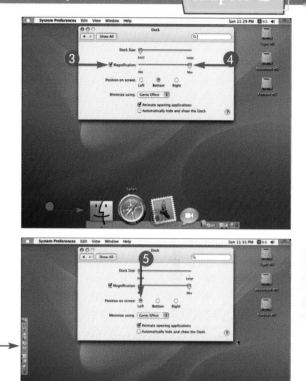

REPOSITION THE DOCK

⑤ Click **Left** or **Right** (◯ changes to ⦿).

● The Dock repositions to the edge of the screen.

(TIPS)

Is there another way that I can adjust the Dock?

Yes. You can also adjust the Dock by holding down `Control` and then clicking the thin vertical line that appears on the Dock. A pop-up menu appears displaying the options available for adjusting the Dock.

Are there any other Dock tricks I should know about?

Yes. You can move the Dock to another position on your Desktop. To do this, press and hold `⌘` + `Shift` and click and drag the Dock by the dividing line to the left, right, or bottom of the screen. The Dock moves in the direction that you drag.

Reveal the Keyboard Viewer

A typical Macintosh keyboard is capable of producing many characters. You can see the possible symbols that your keystrokes produce with the Keyboard Viewer. The Keyboard viewer can be accessed through the System Preferences. It helps you to quickly and easily see examples of all of the available characters in a font.

Reveal the Keyboard Viewer

① In System Preferences, click **International**.

Note: To view System Preferences, see the section "Change the Appearance of the Mac Interface," earlier in this chapter.

The International pane of System Preferences, which is where you can set the language you want to use, appears.

② Click **Input Menu**.

A list of the installed keyboard layouts appears.

③ Click **Keyboard Viewer** (☐ changes to ☑).

④ Click **Show input menu in menu bar** (☐ changes to ☑).

A menu appears adjacent to the clock.

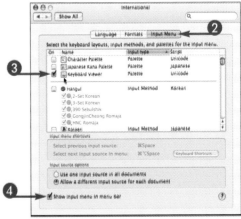

⑤ Click **Show Keyboard Viewer**.

The Keyboard Viewer appears, displaying a virtual keyboard.

⑥ Press any of the modifier keys, such as Control, ⌘, Option, or Shift, to display the available characters on the keyboard.

The floating Keyboard Viewer window intercepts and displays all keystrokes, but it also continues to pass the keystrokes to your foremost application.

TIPS

Why do some keys have missing characters?

The Keyboard Viewer displays the characters specific to the currently selected font. Not all fonts implement all characters. The Keyboard Viewer helps you to quickly determine whether you should use a specific font for a project or not. You can switch fonts through the Font pop-up menu, which is located at the bottom-left corner of the Keyboard Viewer.

How do I deactivate the Keyboard menu?

You can deactivate the Keyboard menu by opening the International pane of the System Preferences and deselecting the **Show input menu in menu bar** option (☑ changes to ☐).

Set Default Behaviors of CDs and DVDs

When you insert a CD or DVD, your Mac is programmed to respond to this action in different ways, depending on what you have told it to do. For example, it may launch a related application, or it may ask you what you want it to do with the disc. You can control the default behavior by selecting settings in the CDs & DVDs pane of System Preferences.

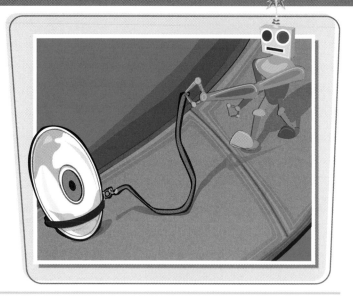

Set Default Behaviors of CDs and DVDs

SET BEHAVIORS

1 In System Preferences, click **CDs & DVDs**.

The **CDs & DVDs** pane opens.

2 Click 🔁 and select **Open Finder**.

Blank CDs will now appear in the Finder just like any other disc.

LAUNCH ITUNES

1 Click 🔁 and select **Open iTunes**.

This setting assumes that you want to burn a music CD upon inserting a blank CD.

LAUNCH IDVD

① Click ⬚ and select **Open iDVD**.

This setting assumes that you want to burn a video DVD upon inserting a blank DVD.

CDs & DVDs

Show All

When you insert a blank CD: 🎵 Open iTunes
When you insert a blank DVD: 📀 Open iDVD ◀—①
When you insert a music CD: 🎵 Open iTunes
When you insert a picture CD:
When you insert a video DVD: 📀 Open DVD Player

DECIDE ON DISC INSERTION

① Click ⬚ and select **Ask what to do**.

Your Mac asks you what you want it to do each time you insert a DVD.

CDs & DVDs

Show All

When you insert a blank CD: 🎵 Open iTunes
When you insert a blank DVD: Ask what to do ◀—①
When you insert a music CD: 🎵 Open iTunes
When you insert a picture CD:
When you insert a video DVD: 📀 Open DVD Player

TIPS

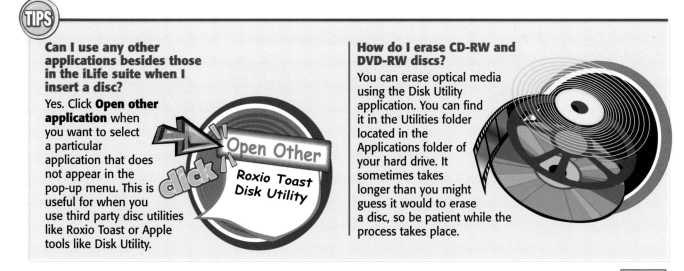

Can I use any other applications besides those in the iLife suite when I insert a disc?

Yes. Click **Open other application** when you want to select a particular application that does not appear in the pop-up menu. This is useful for when you use third party disc utilities like Roxio Toast or Apple tools like Disk Utility.

How do I erase CD-RW and DVD-RW discs?

You can erase optical media using the Disk Utility application. You can find it in the Utilities folder located in the Applications folder of your hard drive. It sometimes takes longer than you might guess it would to erase a disc, so be patient while the process takes place.

Most desktop Macs use separate CRT and flatscreen displays, while laptops, iMacs, and eMacs have built-in displays. You can adjust the display settings using the Displays pane of the System Preferences window. The display settings let you change the dimensions of your desktop in pixels, the number of colors that your monitor displays, and other settings to calibrate your display.

Adjust the Display Settings

SET THE DISPLAY RESOLUTION

1 In System Preferences, click **Displays**.

Note: *To view System Preferences, see the section "Change the Appearance of the Mac Interface," earlier in this chapter.*

The Displays pane opens.

2 Click a dimension in the **Resolutions** list.

The display switches to the resolution you selected.

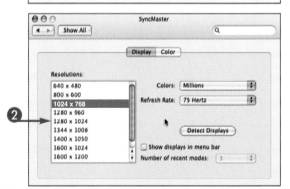

CALIBRATE THE DISPLAY

1 Click **Color**.

● If your Mac has a matching display driver profile installed, it appears in the Display Profile list; click it to select it.

If your display does not appear in the list, proceed to the next step.

2 Click **Calibrate**.

The Display Calibrator Assistant launches.

3 Click **Continue** to begin calibrating your display.

The Display Calibrator Assistant guides you through the calibration process and then calibrates the display upon completion of the setup.

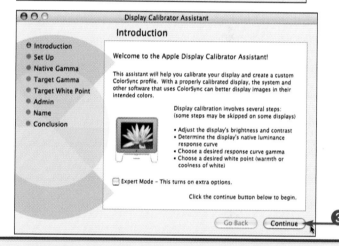

TIPS

Why do I need to calibrate my display?

When you calibrate your display, you increase the chances that graphics will appear the same to you as they do to others. It also increases the likelihood that any printing that you do will look as similar as possible to what you see on the display. You can even purchase a more advanced calibration software and hardware setup for higher-end requirements. These types of system preserve color accuracy with the utmost precision, thus allowing you to get very accurate results. This is primarily meant for those that require professional level color printing.

What happens when I connect an additional display to my Mac?

When you connect multiple displays to your Mac, the Display pane of the System Preferences window changes, adding extra settings for each additional display as well as a Geometry setting to tell where each monitor is positioned. Some Macs have so-called "dual" video cards, which means that they can drive two different monitors. If your Mac has only one video card, you Mac may require an additional card to connect additional displays.

Schedule Sleep

The Mac OS is an energy-conscious operating system. With the Energy Saver pane of System Preferences, you can adjust settings that put your computer to sleep, cause the display to sleep, and even spin down the hard drive. This is especially good news for laptop users, as laptops benefit from extended battery life. You can also schedule start-up and shutdown times.

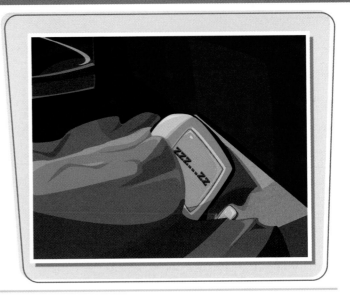

Schedule Sleep

SET COMPUTER DISPLAY SLEEP TIME

① In System Preferences, click **Energy Saver**.

Note: To view System Preferences, see the section "Change the Appearance of the Mac Interface," earlier in this chapter.

The Energy Saver pane opens.

② Click and drag 🔽 to adjust the computer sleep timer.

The computer sleeps after a period of inactivity based on this setting.

③ Click and drag 🔽 to adjust the display sleep timer.

The display sleeps after a period of inactivity based on this setting.

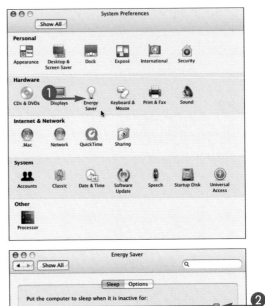

SCHEDULE START-UP AND SHUTDOWN TIMES

1 Click **Schedule**.

2 Select the **Start up or wake** option (☑ changes to ☐).

3 Click **Every Day**.

4 Type **7:00 AM** or click the little arrows to set the time.

The computer will now start at 7:00 a.m. every day.

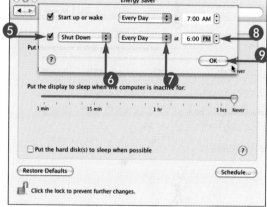

5 Click this option (☐ changes to ☑).

6 Click 🔽 and select **Shut Down**.

7 Click 🔽 and select **Every Day**.

8 Type **6:00 PM** or click the little arrows to set the time.

9 Click **OK**.

The computer will now shut down at 6:00 p.m. every day.

TIPS

What happens when the computer attempts a scheduled shutdown with unsaved documents open?

If you have unsaved documents open in any application, a scheduled shutdown will not proceed to its conclusion until you tell your Mac what to do with the unsaved documents. This works the same as when you try to manually shut down a Mac with unsaved documents. The computer will not shut down and you will not lose your data.

How do I put the computer to sleep manually, and how do I wake it up?

To put the computer to sleep manually, click **Sleep** in the 🍎 menu. To wake up a sleeping Mac, press any key or move the mouse. If you use a laptop, you can put your Mac to sleep by closing the computer. For more information, see Chapter 1.

Adjust the Keyboard and Mouse

You can adjust the repeat rate of the keyboard as well as the tracking and click rate of the mouse. You can make these adjustments through the Keyboard and Mouse pane of the System Preferences window. You can also use a USB mouse with left and right-clicking capabilities.

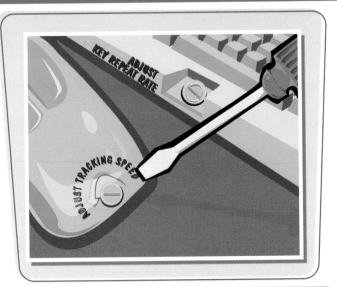

Adjust the Keyboard and Mouse

SET THE KEYBOARD REPEAT RATE

1 In System Preferences click **Keyboard & Mouse**.

Note: To view System Preferences, see the section "Change the Appearance of the Mac Interface," earlier in this chapter.

The Keyboard & Mouse pane opens.

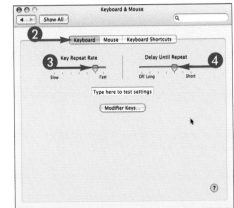

2 Click **Keyboard**.

3 Click and drag ⬇ to specify how rapidly letters appear on the screen as you type them.

4 Click and drag ⬇ to specify how long the Mac OS waits before a depressed key produces multiple characters on the screen.

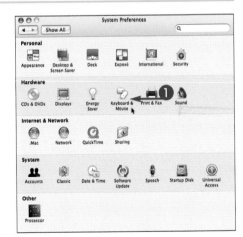

SET THE MOUSE TRACKING AND DOUBLE-CLICK SPEED

1 Click **Mouse**.

2 Click and drag ▣ to specify how fast the mouse moves on the screen.

3 Click and drag ▣ to specify how rapidly you must click the mouse twice to initiate a double-click.

● You can test the effectiveness of your settings by double-clicking in this box.

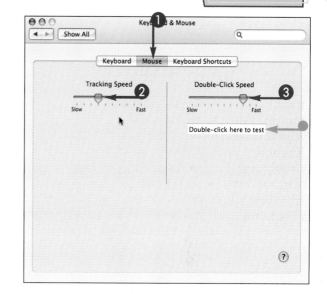

TIPS

I have a USB mouse with two buttons on it. Will it work with my Mac.

Any USB-compatible mouse should work with your Mac. This includes the so-called right-click that you normally find with a Windows-based mouse. Clicking the second mouse button provides the same functionality as `Control`+click.

Do I really need a two-button mouse?

The Mac OS is designed with a one-button mouse or trackpad in mind. There are no functions that are unavailable to a one-button mouse. Some people find that a multi-button mouse saves them time since the extra buttons perform important shortcut functions. You do not need one, but you may like one, especially if you do not like to use both hands to access contextual menus.

Set the Date and Time

Nearly every operation that you perform on a computer is recorded in detail using the date and time of the computer's clock. You may also want to know the time yourself. You can set the date and time by hand or let your Mac do it for you by connecting to a time server on the Internet.

Set the Date and Time

SET TIME AUTOMATICALLY

1 Click **System Preferences**.

2 Click **Date & Time**.

The Date & Time settings appear.

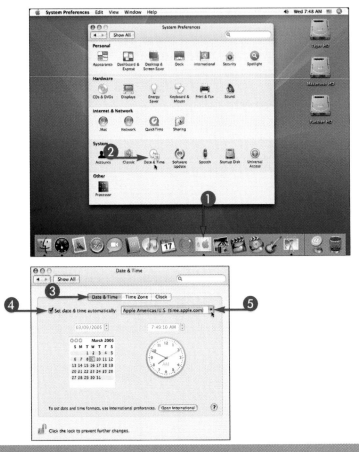

3 Click **Date & Time**.

4 Click **Set Date & Time automatically**
   (☑ changes to ☐).

5 Click here and select the time server that is geographically closest to you.

Your Mac sets the date and time automatically from the Internet.

Note: *This setting works best if you have an "always-on" Internet connection, like cable or DSL.*

MANUALLY SET THE DATE

1 Uncheck **Set Date & Time automatically**
(☐ changes to ☑).

2 Click here and type the current month's
corresponding number.

3 Click here and type the current day of the month.

4 Click here and type in the year.

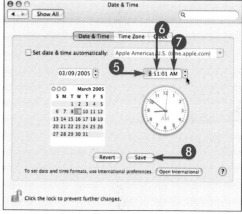

MANUALLY SET THE TIME

5 Click here and type in the hour.

6 Click here and type in a value for minutes.

7 Click an arrow button to select **AM** or **PM**.

8 Click **Save**.

The date and time settings for the computer change.

TIPS

How does my Mac know where I am to set the time automatically?

Your Mac knows your location based on the time zone that you set in the **Time Zone** tab of the Date and Time Preferences Pane. You also may have set the time zone the first time that you used your installation of Mac OS X Tiger. You can set the time zone by clicking on the map or by choosing a city from the **Closest City** pop-up menu.

If my Mac can set its time automatically, why would I want to set it manually?

To set the date and time automatically, your Mac requires a connection to the Internet. If you do not have a network connection, you can still set the clock manually. This option is particularly useful for laptop users, since they often do not have a network connection. Further, laptop users are more likely to travel and may wish to change the clock to match the local time.

Customize the Appearance of the Clock

You can alter how your Mac displays the clock by changing settings in the Date & Time pane of the System Preferences. You can toggle the appearance of the clock between analog and digital faces and even move it around in a floating window. You can also customize the format of the time, choosing to optionally display AM or PM, the day of the week, and adjust the transparency of the clock window.

Customize the Appearance of the Clock

VIEW THE CLOCK IN THE MENU BAR OR IN A WINDOW

① Open **Date & Time** in the System Preferences.

② Click **Clock**.

③ Click **Show the date and time** (☑ changes to ☐).

④ Click **Menu Bar** (◯ changes to ◉).

● The clock appears in the **Menu Bar**.

⑤ Click **Window** (◯ changes to ◉).

● The clock appears in a floating window.

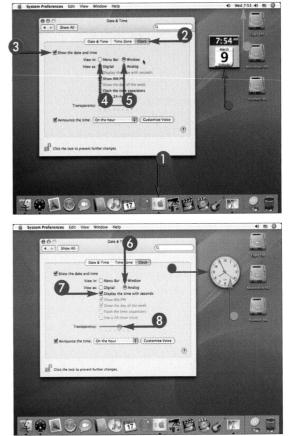

CHANGE THE ANALOG CLOCK STYLE

⑥ Click **Analog** (◯ changes to ◉).

● An analog clock face appears in the floating window.

⑦ Click **Display the time with seconds** (☑ changes to ☐).

● An animated second hand appears on the clock face.

⑧ Click and drag ◈.

As you move the slider, the transparency of the clock window changes to reveal elements behind it.

CHANGE THE DIGITAL CLOCK FORMAT

⑨ Click **Menu Bar** (⚪ changes to ⚫).

The clock reappears in the menu bar.

⑩ Click **Digital** to give the clock a digital appearance (⚪ changes to ⚫).

● These options toggle the AM/PM indicator, day of the week, and flashing colon.

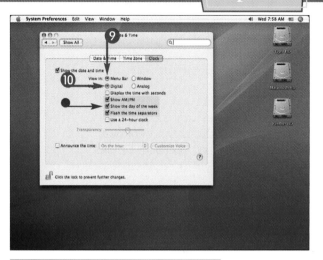

HEAR THE TIME

① Click **Announce the Time** (☐ changes to ☑).

② Click 🔽 and select a time interval.

This example shows **On the half hour** selected.

Your computer speaks the time at the chosen interval.

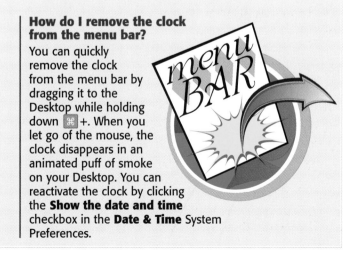

How can I move the clock from one location to another in the Menu bar?

You can reposition the clock in the right side of the menu bar by pressing ⌘ and clicking and dragging it to a new location. Keep in mind that if there are no other elements in the right-hand corner of the menu bar, the clock will not move.

How do I remove the clock from the menu bar?

You can quickly remove the clock from the menu bar by dragging it to the Desktop while holding down ⌘+. When you let go of the mouse, the clock disappears in an animated puff of smoke on your Desktop. You can reactivate the clock by clicking the **Show the date and time** checkbox in the **Date & Time** System Preferences.

Make Your Mac Speak

One of the most memorable demonstrations of the first Macintosh was its ability to speak. Today's Mac can speak any text you feed it, in a variety of voices and at different rates. To begin speaking text, you should set the default voice. Other applications use the default voice for speech production.

SET THE DEFAULT VOICE

1 In System Preferences, click **Speech**.

Note: To view System Preferences, see the section "Change the Appearance of the Mac Interface."

The Speech pane opens.

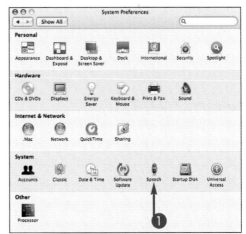

2 Click **Text to Speech**.

3 Click ⬍ and select **Victoria**.

4 Click **Play**.

The computer recites a demonstration sentence in the Victoria voice.

5 Click and drag 🔘 to control the speed of speech.

6 Click **Play**.

Your Mac speaks the same demonstration sentence, but at the chosen rate.

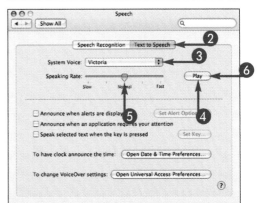

ACTIVATE SPOKEN ALERTS

① Click **Announce when alerts are displayed**
(☑ changes to ☐).

Whenever an alert window opens on the screen,
your Mac reads aloud the alert.

② Click **Announce when an application requires
your attention** (☑ changes to ☐).

③ Click **Set Alert Options**.

The **Alert Options** sheet opens.

④ Click ▣ and select a voice.

Your Mac reads the alerts using the Bruce voice.

⑤ Click and drag ▣ to adjust the amount of time your
computer waits to speak an alert.

⑥ Click **OK** to dismiss the sheet and apply the settings.

TIPS

**How can I make the Mac speak some
text of my choosing?**

In many application menus, you can access
the Services menu item. This menu item
contains functions that you can use
with multiple applications.
First, select some text
from a document in an
application like TextEdit.
Then, click **Services**. Finally,
click **Speech**. This causes
the Mac to speak selected
text using the default voice.
The Mac will even recognize
punctuation, pausing for commas
and inflecting for questions.

Professor Mac
speaking on the topic
"Our Friend, The Tiger"

Can I listen to Web pages?

You can have your Mac read web pages to
you by selecting all text in a Web page.
Then, click **Services**. Finally, click **Speech**.
The Mac reads the web page
text. Your results may vary
depending on the layout
of the Web page, as
elements like menus
and advertisements
might be read, too.

Control Your Mac with Voice Commands

Mac OS X Tiger can recognize and respond to your spoken commands. You can customize the phrases that your Mac understands with command sets so you can control different applications. Your Mac can also understand the set of commands in the Speakable Items folder.

ACTIVATE SPEECH RECOGNITION

① In System Preferences, click **Speech**.

② Click **Speech Recognition**.

③ Click **On** (○ changes to ◉).

● Speech Recognition activates and the feedback window opens, indicating the audio level of the sound it hears.

④ Click **Change Key**.

A sheet opens prompting you to press a key which will be used to activate listening.

⑤ Press a listening key.

⑥ Click **OK**.

The listening key sheet closes.

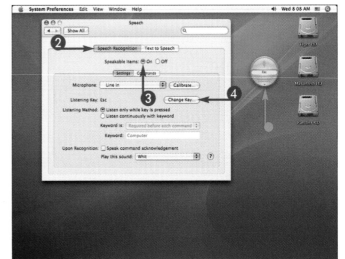

WORK WITH SPOKEN COMMANDS

① Click **Speech Recognition**.

② Click **Commands**.

③ Click **Address Book** (☐ changes to ☑).

Speech Recognition begins listening for names in your address book.

Note: A command set is a group of commands that you can speak and to which the Mac will respond.

④ Click **Configure**.

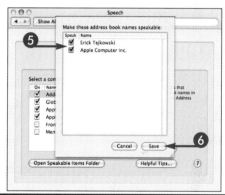

A sheet opens revealing speakable names in the Address Book.

⑤ Click the names you want to make speakable (☑ changes to ☐).

⑥ Click **Save**.

The Address Book sheet closes.

TIPS

What types of speakers can my Mac understand?

Your Mac can understand speakers of U.S. English. It is designed for adult speakers only, not children. You may encounter some difficulties getting recognition if you have a particularly marked accent. Standard U.S. English speakers fare the best. The speech recognition in Tiger is equally adept at recognizing male and female speakers.

What can improve my computer's speech recognition performance?

Macs are relatively good at recognizing your utterances if you heed a few precautions beforehand. First, recognition will only be as good as the microphone that you use. Built-in microphones may suffice, but you will get far better performance using a high-quality external microphone. Also important is the positioning of the microphone. Try to keep the microphone three to fives inches from your mouth. Finally, how you speak can make a huge difference in your Mac's ability to process the speech. Speak in a clear, relaxed, and natural fashion for best results. Try not to slur words together, mumble, or speak too rapidly. All of these factors have a distinct impact on your computer's speech recognition performance.

CHAPTER

4

Completing Everyday Tasks

Tiger has many useful tools that make daily tasks simpler and quicker to complete. This chapter describes how to use Address Book, iCal, Spotlight, TextEdit, and Stickies to make frequent tasks easy.

Add a Contact to the Address Book

You can keep track of family, friends, and business contacts by storing their names, addresses, and telephone numbers in the Address Book. Besides having a convenient place for all of this information, Tiger uses it to automatically complete forms on web pages and help you address emails with only a few keystrokes. You can also print the contact information on address labels.

Add a Contact to the Address Book

LAUNCH ADDRESS BOOK

① Click **Address Book**.

The Address Book application launches.

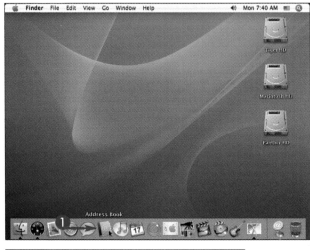

CREATE A NEW CONTACT CARD

① Click **All**.

② Click the Plus sign (⊞).

● Address Book creates a new contact.

③ Type a first name in the **First** field.

④ Type a last name in the **Last** field.

⑤ Click on and then type a telephone number into the home **Phone** field.

⑥ Click here and type an email address.

⑦ Click **Edit**.

The name and contact information are added to the Contact Card.

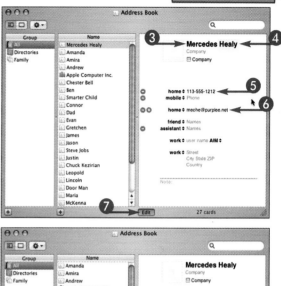

EDIT A CONTACT CARD

① Click a contact card from the Name list.

Address Book displays the contact card.

② Click **Edit**.

Address Book enters editing mode.

③ Click here and type in an address for the contact.

④ Click **Edit.**

Address Book adds the address to the existing contact.

TIPS

Can I use information from Address Book in other applications?

Some applications incorporate Address Book features. Mail, for example, permits you to address emails based on information stored in Address Book. Safari also permits you to auto-complete forms using the data from the Me card in Address Book.

How can I view a map of a contact in Address Book?

You can view a map of a contact on the Internet by clicking and holding the label that precedes a contact's address. Click **Map** in the pop-up menu that opens to view a map of the address in a Web browser.

Organize Contacts

A group is a collection of contacts in Address Book. You can put contact cards into groups to better organize your Address Book and to more easily email multiple recipients at once. Because groups do not affect individual contact information, you can add and delete groups without fear of losing data. You can also add a photograph to contact information, so you can quickly identify contacts and group members visually.

Organize Contacts

CREATE A GROUP

① In Address Book, click ⊞.

Address Book creates a group.

② Type a name for the group.

③ Press **Return**.

Address Book adds the name to the group.

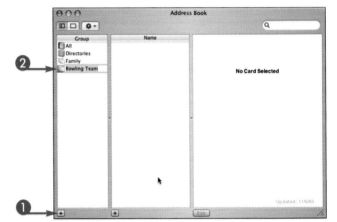

ADD CARDS TO A GROUP

① Click **All**.

Address Book displays all contacts.

② Click and drag a contact to a group.

Address Book adds the contact to the group.

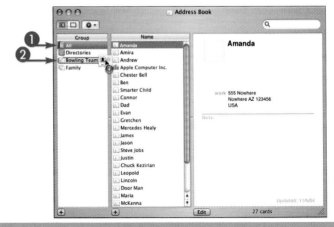

REMOVE A GROUP

1 Select a group.

2 Click **Edit**.

3 Click **Delete Group**.

Address Book removes the group.

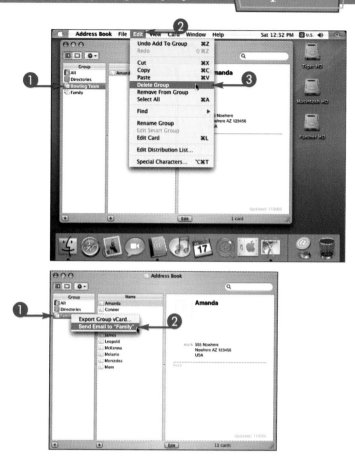

SEND AN EMAIL TO A GROUP

1 Press Control and click the name of a group.

A contextual menu appears.

2 Click **Send Email to "Group Name"**.

A new email opens with addresses for each contact in the group.

Note: To learn more about using email, see Chapter 8.

 TIPS

If I remove a contact from a group, does it permanently remove the contact from the Address Book?

Deleting a contact from a group (other than All) does not remove it from the Address Book. The only way to remove a contact from the Address Book is to delete it from the All group.

How do I insert a picture of a contact into the contact's card?

You can double-click the head shot adjacent to the contact's name. An image-editing window opens where you can insert a photo of the contact using drag and drop. You can also insert a photo for a contact by clicking the camera button in the image-editing window, or you can click the Choose button to select a image file on your hard drive.

Print Address Labels

You can print address labels for contacts to simplify your mailing list tasks. Address Book provides templates for many different commercially available labels. You can also change the mailing label dimensions to print at custom sizes. In addition to labels, Address Book can print contact lists, complete with photographs of members in the list.

Print Address Labels

CHOOSE CONTACTS

① Select a group.

Address Book displays the names in that group.

② Select the contacts that you want to include in the mailing list by pressing ⌘ and clicking each contact name or Shift-click to select multiple contacts.

PREPARE A PRINT JOB

① Click **File**.

② Click **Print**.

The Print dialog box appears.

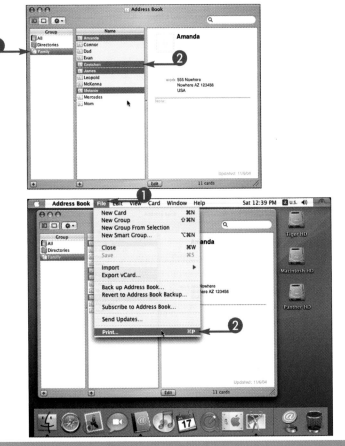

③ Choose **Mailing Labels** from the Style pop-up menu.

④ Click **Layout**.

⑤ Click 🔽 and select **5161** or whatever Avery label style you require.

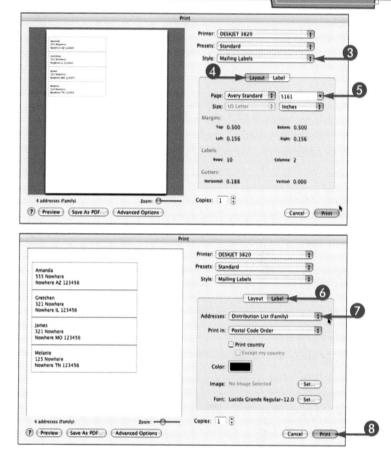

⑥ Click **Label**.

⑦ Click 🔽 and select **Distribution List**.

Address Book prints labels for the selected addresses.

⑧ Click **Print**.

Address Book prints the labels.

TIPS

How do I print a list of contacts instead of mailing labels?

Click **Lists** in the Style pop-up menu to print a list of contacts. You can even print photos of contacts in the listing. Click **Print** to print the contact list.

Avery does not make my labels. How do I define a custom mailing label size?

In the **Page** pop-up menu of the **Layout** tab, click **Define Custom**. You can designate **Margins**, **Labels**, and **Gutters** in a custom layout.

Perform Common Numerical Conversions

The Calculator application in Mac OS X Tiger is more sophisticated than a typical desktop calculator. It has two modes, one for basic use and the other for scientific use. You can calculate many different unit conversions with Calculator, including weight and temperature. You can also adjust the numerical precision of the results that Calculator displays.

Perform Common Numerical Conversions

CONVERT POUNDS TO KILOGRAMS

1 Launch Calculator.

Calculator is located in the Applications folder.

2 Type a weight in pounds that you want to convert.

This example converts 150 pounds.

3 Click **Convert**.

4 Click **Weights and Masses**.

The Conversion sheet opens with Weights and Masses selected in the Convert pop-up menu.

5 Click ⬍ and select **US Pound**.

6 Click ⬍ and select **Kilogram**.

7 Click **OK**.

Calculator displays the results of the conversion in kilograms.

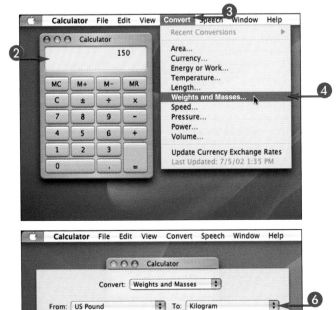

CONVERT CELSIUS TO FAHRENHEIT

① Type a temperature measured in Celsius that you would like to convert.

② Click **Convert**.

③ Click **Temperature**.

The Conversion sheet opens with Temperature selected in the Convert pop-up menu.

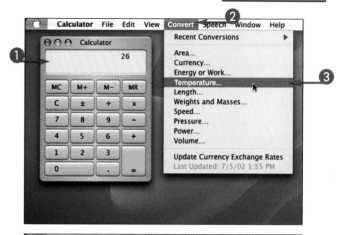

④ Click **Celsius**.

⑤ Click **Fahrenheit**.

⑥ Click **OK**.

Calculator displays the temperature in degrees Fahrenheit.

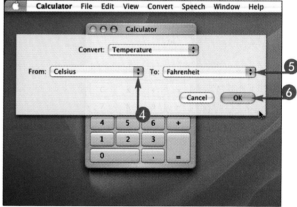

 TIPS

The Calculator application shown in the pictures looks different than the one on my screen. Why is mine smaller than the one pictured in this chapter?

Calculator has three modes: Basic, Advanced, and Programmer. The Basic mode displays numbers and basic arithmetic functions. Advanced mode expands the Calculator interface horizontally and displays scientific functions. Programmer mode includes numeric functions and tools appropriate for computer programmers. Its interface is also larger than the Basic mode interface. You can switch modes using the View menu.

My results have too many digits after the decimal point. How do I limit the precision?

Precision tells you the number of digits after the decimal point. You can adjust the precision of values that Calculator displays. In the View menu, click Precision to reveal a submenu displaying values between 0 and 16. Choose the precision value that corresponds to the number of digits of precision you desire.

Calculate Currency Exchange Rates

You can calculate currency exchange rates with the Calculator application. You can also download up-to-the-minute currency exchange-rate data from the Internet, so you can be sure that the calculations are timely. Because this sort of information changes frequently, Calculator requires that you have an Internet connection to retrieve the exchange-rate data.

Calculate Currency Exchange Rates

CONVERT DOLLARS TO EUROS

① In Calculator, click **Convert**.

② Click **Update Currency Exchange Rates**.

Calculator connects to the Internet and downloads new currency exchange-rate data.

③ Type the number of dollars you want to convert.

④ Click **Convert**.

⑤ Click **Currency**.

The Currency Conversion dialog box opens.

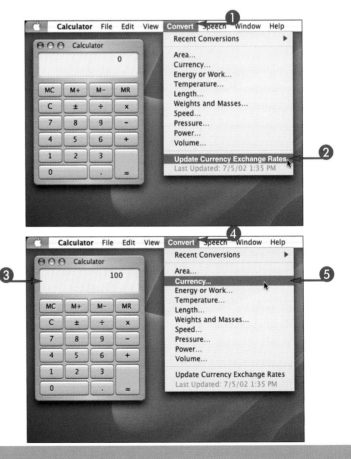

6 Click ⬍ and select **U.S. dollar**.

7 Click ⬍ and select **Euro**.

8 Click **OK**.

Calculator displays the conversion in Euros.

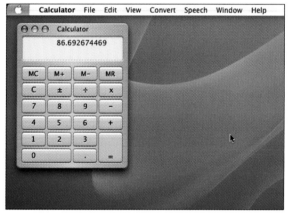

TIPS

How can I view the numbers that I have converted so far?

Click **Show Paper Tape** in the **View** menu to see a textual representation of all recent Calculator data entry. You can copy the data from the paper tape to the clipboard in the **Edit** menu. You can also print the data by clicking **Print Tape** in the **File** menu.

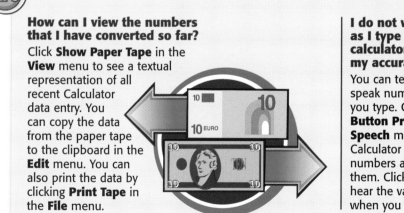

I do not want to look at the screen as I type numbers into the calculator. What can improve my accuracy?

You can tell Calculator to speak numbers for you as you type. Click **Speak Button Pressed** in the **Speech** menu to cause Calculator to speak numbers as you enter them. Click **Speak Total** to hear the value that appears when you click ▣.

Track Your Schedule

You can track important dates and times in your schedule with iCal. iCal is an application that lets you lay out calendars visually. You can add dates, such as holidays, or remove the dates that you do not want on your calendar.

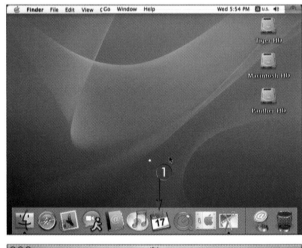

Track Your Schedule

CREATE A NEW CALENDAR

1. Click the **iCal** icon.

   The iCal application launches.

2. Click ⊞.

   A new calendar appears in the Calendars list with its title highlighted, indicating that you can change it.

3. Give the calendar a name by typing it in the Calendars list.

4. Press Return.

ADD AN EVENT TO A CALENDAR

1. Select a calendar from the Calendars list.

2. Click **Month**.

   A monthly calendar appears.

3. Click ◀ or ▶ to display the desired month.

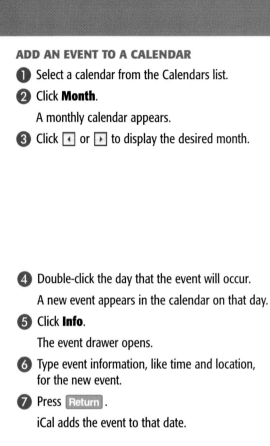

4. Double-click the day that the event will occur.

   A new event appears in the calendar on that day.

5. Click **Info**.

   The event drawer opens.

6. Type event information, like time and location, for the new event.

7. Press Return.

   iCal adds the event to that date.

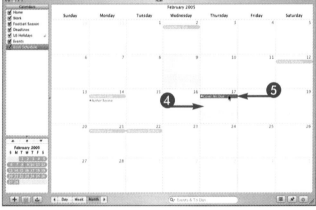

TIPS

How do I remove an event from a specific date?

You simply click to select the event that you want to delete from a particular date. Then press Delete to remove it from the calendar.

How do I schedule blocks of time during a particular day?

Scheduling blocks of time helps you organize a day's events. Click either the **Day** or **Week** button at the bottom of the calendar to view a calendar of days or weeks respectively. You can assign blocks of time to any date when the calendar displays in either of these modes. To assign a block of time, click the starting time and drag downward until the desired block of time is selected.

Subscribe to a Calendar

You can subscribe to free calendars on the Internet, and iCal will display the calendars for you. These calendars display useful information like holidays and important dates. When you are finished using a calendar to which you have subscribed, you can cancel the subscription by deleting the calendar.

Subscribe to a Calendar

TYPE A URL

1 In iCal, click **Calendar**.

2 Click **Subscribe**.

The Subscribe sheet opens.

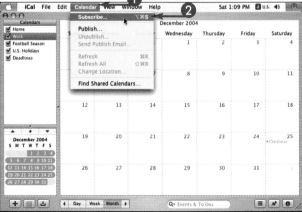

3 Type the URL of a calendar Web site.

This example uses webcal://ical.mac.com/ical/US32Holidays.ics, an Apple site that lists U.S. holidays.

To find other available calendars type **www.apple.com/ical/library** in a Web browser.

Note: To find this Web site and others, see Chapter 8.

4 Click **Subscribe**.

iCal subscribes you to the calendar.

VIEW A CALENDAR SUBSCRIPTION

1 Click the name of the Calendar to which you subscribe.

The calendar appears.

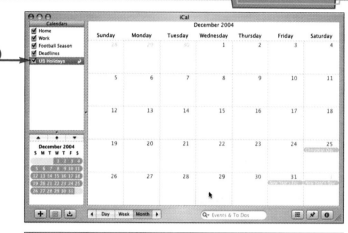

2 Click **Month**.

iCal displays the holidays in the current month.

3 Click ▸.

iCal displays the holidays in the following month.

TIPS

How do I cancel a calendar subscription?

To cancel a calendar subscription, you simply click the calendar that you want to cancel in the Sidebar, and then press Delete.

Where can I find other calendars to which I can subscribe?

The Internet has a wealth of calendars to which you can subscribe. One of the best Web sites is **http://icalshare.com**. Besides national holidays, you can subscribe to calendars that list sports schedules, upcoming movie releases, television events, celebrity birthdays, and many more.

If you subscribe to a service like .Mac, you can publish your own calendars for others to view. By publishing a calendar, other people in your organization can subscribe to the same calendar and stay current. You can unpublish a calendar at any time, such as when it becomes outdated.

Publish a Calendar

PUBLISH A CALENDAR

① In iCal, select a calendar to publish.

② Click **Calendar**.

③ Click **Publish**.

The Publish sheet appears.

④ Type a name for the calendar.

⑤ Click ⬦ and select **.Mac**.

Note: This step requires you to have a .Mac account.

⑥ Click **Publish.**

● iCal publishes the calendar in your .Mac Web space.

Note: To learn more about .Mac, see Chapter 8.

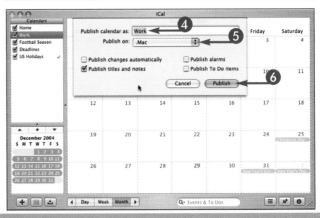

UNPUBLISH A CALENDAR

1 Select a calendar to unpublish.

2 Click **Calendar**.

3 Click **Unpublish**.

iCal prompts you to confirm the action.

4 Click **Unpublish**.

iCal unpublishes the calendar.

TIPS

I do not have a .Mac account. What other options exist for me to publish a calendar?

You can publish calendars if you have access to a WebDAV-enabled Web server. Ask your system administrator or ISP whether this service is available.

Once I publish a calendar, how can I let other people know about it?

There are many excellent Web sites that list publicly available iCal calendars. One of the most popular sites, **http://icalshare. com**, even describes how Windows and Linux users can subscribe to your calendars.

You can use the bundled application TextEdit as your primary word processor. You can type and format text in TextEdit, as well as add pictures to documents. Besides performing the usual tasks of many larger and more expensive word processors, TextEdit can also open and read files from other popular word processors.

Write a Report with TextEdit

LAUNCH TEXTEDIT

1. In the Finder, press ⌘ + Shift + A.

   The Applications folder opens.

2. Double-click **TextEdit**.

   The TextEdit application launches.

SET THE FONT

1. Type some text in a TextEdit document.

② Click and drag to select the text.

③ Click **Format**.

④ Click **Font**.

⑤ Click **Show Fonts**.

The Font panel appears.

⑥ Click a font in the list of available fonts.

The selected text in the document changes to reflect the font choice.

⑦ Click to select a font size.

● The selected text in the document changes size to reflect the size choice.

TIPS

Can I place pictures in a TextEdit document?

You can add a picture to your text by clicking and dragging a picture file from the Finder into the TextEdit document. For this to work, however, you must ensure that the document is in Rich Text format. You can find the Rich Text Format setting in the Format menu.

You can also drag and drop pictures into TextEdit from Preview and other drag-and-drop-compatible applications.

Can other word processors open documents that I create with TextEdit?

TextEdit documents are compatible with most popular word processors. Because TextEdit can save files as RTF (Rich Text Format) and DOC (Microsoft Word Document), TextEdit works well with others. Microsoft Word can open RTF and DOC files and other word processors often support RTF.

Working with Images

Tiger gives you all the tools you need to import digital images from a camera, view those images, organize them into photo albums, and edit them. This chapter describes how to use Preview, QuickTime Player, and iPhoto to work with images.

View Images
with Preview

Preview is an image viewer
application that accompanies
the default installation of Mac
OS X Tiger. You can view
different types of image files
with Preview as well as rotate
pictures and preview animatons.

View Images with Preview

OPEN AN IMAGE

① In the Finder, click **Go**.

② Click **Applications**.

A Finder window opens listing the contents of the
Applications folder.

③ Double-click **Preview**.

The Preview application launches.

④ Click **File**.

⑤ Click **Open**.

The Open dialog box appears.

⑥ Click an image file.

⑦ Click **Open**.

Preview opens the image and displays it.

Can I rotate an image in Preview?

While viewing an image in Preview, you can rotate it counterclockwise in 90-degree increments by pressing ⌘ + L. Press ⌘ + R to rotate clockwise in 90-degree increments.

Can I view animated image files like GIF in Preview?

Preview can display animated sequences in common animated graphics formats like GIF. To view an animated GIF, open it as you would open any other image file and click the **Start Animation** button in the toolbar.

Export Images with Preview

At some point, you may need to convert an image to a different format. You can use Preview to convert images from one file format, like TIFF, to another format, like JPEG.

SAVE A JPEG IMAGE

① In Preview, open an image file.

Note: See the section "View Images with Preview" to launch Preview.

② Click **File**.

③ Click **Save As**.

The Save As window opens.

④ Type a name for the new file.

⑤ Click 🔽 and select **JPEG**.

⑥ Click **Save**.

Preview saves the image in JPEG format.

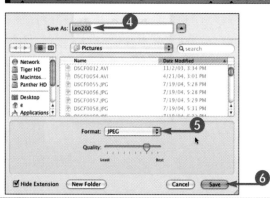

SAVE A TIFF IMAGE

1. In Preview, open an image file.
2. Click **File**.
3. Click **Save As**.

4. Click ⊟ and select **TIFF**.
5. Click **Save**.

Preview saves the file as a TIFF image.

TIPS

Why do so many image file formats exist?

Each file format has a different purpose. Some formats, such as JPEG, are better than others for creating small files that are useful on the Internet. Other formats are better for exchanging with Windows users, such as BMP. Yet other formats are best for maintaining the highest quality at the expense of increased size, such as TIFF.

Where are some of these image file formats used?

BMP	Common on Microsoft Windows
JPEG	Smaller file size at expense of quality commonly used in digital cameras
PDF	Portable Document Format; useful in Preview and for exchanging with Windows, Linux, and UNIX users
PNG	Commonly used on the web
TIFF	High quality format; sometimes used in digital cameras

View Images with QuickTime Player

Despite its connotation with playing movies, QuickTime Player also works well as an image viewer. You can view a variety of image file formats in QuickTime Player.

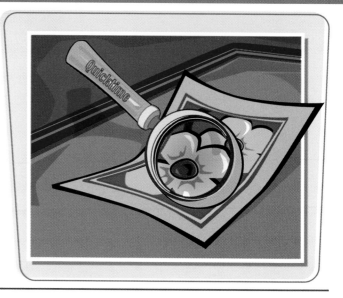

VIEW IMAGES

① In the Dock, click **QuickTime Player**.

QuickTime Player launches.

② Click **File**.

③ Click **Open Movie**.

The Open dialog box appears.

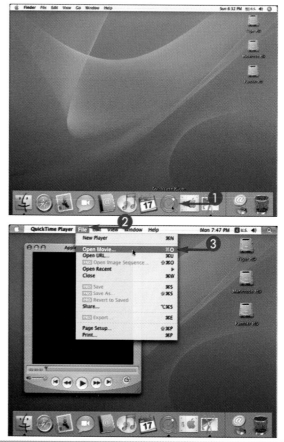

④ Click an image file.

⑤ Click **Open**.

QuickTime Player opens the image file and displays it in a window.

TIPS

How do I zoom images in QuickTime Player?

When viewing an image in QuickTime Player, you can adjust the scale of an image by resizing the window that contains the image. To resize a window, click the green zoom button or click and drag the bottom right corner of the window.

Can I view animated image files like GIF in QuickTime Player?

QuickTime Player can display animated sequences in common animated graphics formats like GIF. To view an animated GIF in QuickTime Player, open it as you would any other image file. To view the individual frames of the animation, press 🔘 or 🔘. To view the animation, click Play.

Apply Effects to Photos in Preview

Preview offers some useful effects that you can apply to printed photos. For example, you can add sepia to a photo to give it an old-fashioned appearance. When you are finished adding effects to your photo, you can either print the image or save it as a PDF for later use.

Apply Effects to Photos in Preview

1 Open a photo in Preview.

Note: To open a photo, see the section "View Images with Preview."

2 Click **File**.

3 Click **Print**.

The Print sheet opens, displaying a preview of the photo.

PRINT A SEPIA-TONE PHOTO

4 Click [▼] and select **Sepia Tone**.

The preview image changes to reflect the new filter.

5 Click the **Print** button.

Preview sends the image to your printer to be printed.

PRINT A COLORIZED PHOTO

6️⃣ Click ⬍ and select **Blue Tone**.

The preview image changes to reflect the new filter.

7️⃣ Click the **Print** button.

Preview sends the image to your printer to be printed.

SAVE A PDF

1️⃣ In the Print sheet, click **PDF**.

A Save dialog box opens.

2️⃣ Type a name for the file.

3️⃣ and click **Save**.

Preview saves the PDF file.

Is Preview the only application that offers these effects?

No. Quartz is the name of the engine that draws elements on the screen. It also provides sophisticated filter effects throughout the operating system. You can access the same Quartz filters in most applications through the Print sheet. Open the Print sheet by clicking **Print** in the **File** menu. Select **Color Sync** in the Print sheet to reveal the Quartz Filter settings in any application that supports printing.

Can I apply multiple effects to an image?

Yes. To apply multiple effects to an image, save the image after applying an effect to it. Then, open the altered image and export it again with another effect.

View Images with iPhoto

The premiere photo application in Mac OS X Tiger is iPhoto. With iPhoto, you can instantly access a variety of images on your hard drive.

View Images with iPhoto

IMPORT IMAGES

1 In the Finder, double-click **iPhoto** in the Applications folder.

Note: To open the Applications folder, see Chapter 1.

2 Click **File**.

3 Click **Add to Library**.

The Import Photos dialog box opens.

4 Click a file that you want to import.

5 Click **Import**.

iPhoto adds the image to the Library.

VIEW IMAGES

6 Click and drag the scrollbar to view all images in the Library.

7 Click and drag the **Zoom slider** ([⬤]).

iPhoto increases the size of images as you drag to the right.

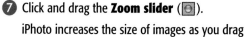

TIPS

Can I import multiple files at once?

In the Import Photos dialog box, you can import multiple images at once by pressing ⌘ and clicking each file that you want to import. Then, click the **Import** button.

SHORT CUT

Why do some images appear jagged and out of focus when I zoom?

If you zoom in on an image too much, you will exceed its dimensions. As soon as you do, iPhoto has to compensate for the pixels that are not in the original image and fills in its best guess. This causes artifacts like blurring and jagged edges. These artifacts do not affect the image file itself.

Export Images with iPhoto

Once you add images to your iPhoto Library, you can export them to some common formats for other uses. You can save images in the JPEG format for sending in emails or posting on a web page. If you do not know how to create a web page, iPhoto can create one of those too. Using QuickTime, you can also create a slideshow movie that displays photos you select.

SAVE AS JPEG

1 In iPhoto, click **Library**.

iPhoto displays the images in the Photo Library.

2 Click a photo to select it.

3 Click **Share**.

4 Click **Export**.

The Export Photos dialog box opens.

5. Click **File Export**.

6. Click ⬍ and select **JPG**.

7. Click **Export**.

The Export sheet appears and prompts you to choose a location for the exported photo.

8. Select a location for the exported photo.

9. Type a name for the file.

10. Click **OK**.

iPhoto exports the image in the file chosen format and location.

TIPS

What else can iPhoto export?

In addition to JPG, iPhoto can export the popular TIFF and PNG formats. You can also export a set of photos for display on Web pages. iPhoto creates the Web pages for you, complete with thumbnail images and links to all images. iPhoto also creates copies of the desired images and places them in an accompanying folder.

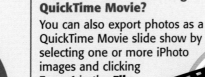

Can I use an iPhoto image in a QuickTime Movie?

You can also export photos as a QuickTime Movie slide show by selecting one or more iPhoto images and clicking **Export** in the **File** menu. In the iPhoto Export window, you can save a QuickTime movie by clicking the QuickTime tab. Adjust the movie's settings and click **Export** to complete the task.

Edit Photos with iPhoto

Besides being a great image viewer, iPhoto offers a number of editing features as well. Without much effort, you can crop an image, adjust its contrast, and convert it to black and white. You can also target changes to specific sections of a photo, instead of the whole thing. If you do not like something along the way, you can undo any changes that you make.

Edit Photos with iPhoto

CONVERT FROM COLOR TO GRAYSCALE

① In iPhoto, click **Library**.

② Click an image to select it.

③ Click **Edit**.

The toolbar displays tools related to image editing.

④ Click the **B & W** button.

The image changes from color to grayscale.

ADJUST BRIGHTNESS AND CONTRAST

1 Open a color image in iPhoto.

2 Click **Adjust**.

The Adjust palette opens.

3 Click and drag the **Brightness** 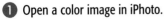 to the right of center.

The image appears brighter.

4 Drag the **Contrast** to the left of center.

iPhoto reduces the contrast of the image.

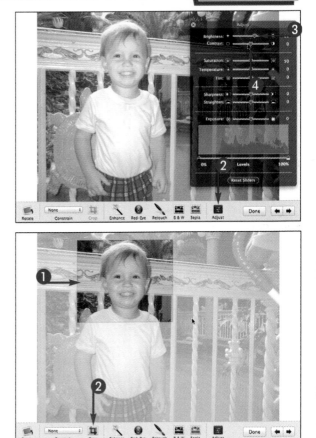

CROP AN IMAGE

1 Click and drag to select the portion of the image that you want to crop.

2 Click the **Crop** button.

iPhoto crops the image to the selection rectangle, discarding anything outside the selection.

Note: *The Constrain pop-up menu and the Crop tool work in tandem when making a selection for cropping.*

TIPS

What should I do if I make a mistake while editing an image?

You can always revert an image in iPhoto. Click **Undo** in the **Edit** menu to undo the last action. Click **Undo** again to undo the last action before that. Once you save and close a file, however, you must click **Revert to Original** in the **Photos** menu to return a photo to its original look.

Can I apply all iPhoto effects to the selected portion of an image instead of the whole image?

You can apply all iPhoto editing effects to either the entire image or only the selected portion of an image. For example, when using the **Red-eye filter**, you should select only the portion of the image where the red eye appears. That way, the rest of the image remains unchanged.

Catalog and Organize Your Photos

iPhoto provides many useful features for working with images, but perhaps the most useful, is its ability to manage large collections of images.

ADD PHOTOS TO A PHOTO ALBUM

1. In iPhoto, click ➕.

   A sheet appears, asking you to type a name for a new album.

2. Type a name for the album.

3. Click **Create**.

● iPhoto creates the new Photo Album.

4. Click **Library**.

   iPhoto displays the images in the Photo Library.

⑤ Press ⌘ and click one or more photos.

iPhoto selects and highlights each photo that you click.

⑥ Drag the selected images from the Photo Library to the new Photo Album.

iPhoto adds the images to the Photo Album.

TIPS

What happens when I remove an image from a Photo Album?

An iPhoto Photo Album is a collection of references to images in the Photo Library. If you select an image in a Photo Album and remove it by pressing Delete, the image reference is removed from the album but remains in the Photo Library.

How do I remove an image from the Library?

To completely remove an image from iPhoto, you must delete it from the Photo Library. First, click **Photo Library** in the Source list on the left. Then, click the image that you want to remove and press Delete.

You can transfer images from a digital camera to your iPhoto Library automatically by using iPhoto's import feature. If you prefer, you can manually add these images in the Finder. Whichever method you choose, you can erase the contents of the camera when you are finished.

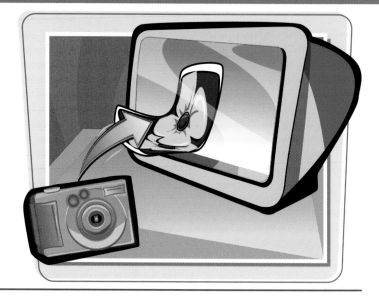

Import Photos from a Camera

① With iPhoto open, connect a digital camera to your Mac.

● The camera appears in the Source list.

② Click **Delete items from camera after importing** (⬜ changes to ☑) to tell iPhoto to erase the photos from the camera after import.

③ Name the Roll of photos that you are importing.

④ Enter a description of the imported photos.

⑤ Click the **Info** button.

● Information about the camera, including the size of all images on the camera, appears below the **Source** list.

⑥ Click the **Import** button.

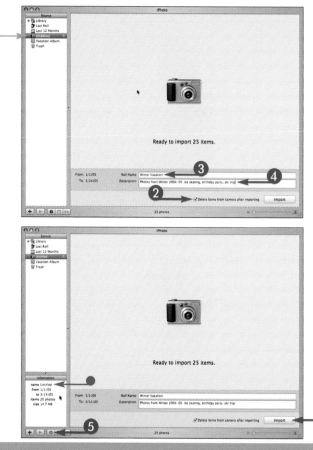

to prompts you to confirm that you want to
te photos from the camera once the import
operation has completed.

⑦ Click **Delete Originals**.

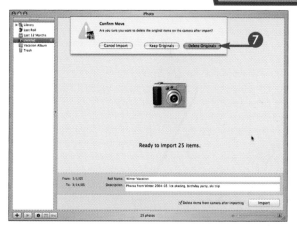

● iPhoto displays a status bar showing the progress of
the importing session.

● To cancel for any reason, click **Stop Import**.

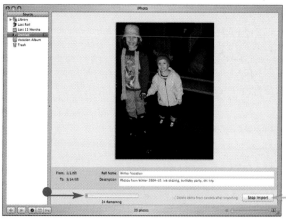

TIP

Do I have to use iPhoto to retrieve photos from my camera?
You can also use the Finder to retrieve images from a camera, but
first you must disable autostarting iPhoto in the Preferences of
the Image Capture application. If you do not, iPhoto launches
every time your Mac detects that you have connected a
camera. To disable autostarting, launch the Image Capture
application and click **Preferences** in the **Image Capture**
menu. Click **None** in the **When a camera is connected,
open** popup menu.

To transfer images from the camera, quit iPhoto, connect a
camera, and power up the device. The camera appears on
the Desktop as a disk, just like any other disk. Click and drag
the files from the camera disk to a folder on your hard drive.
You can also delete images from the camera by moving them to
the Trash and emptying it.

Email a Picture Using iPhoto

Photographs are much more fun if you can share them. With iPhoto, you can share images with friends and family through email.

Email a Picture Using iPhoto

① In iPhoto, click **Library**.

② Select a photo that you want to email.

③ Click the **Email** button.

The Mail Photo window appears.

④ Click ⬍ and select the desired photo size.

Options include Large (1280x960 pixels), Medium (640x480 pixels), Small (320x240 pixels), and Full Size where the dimensions match the dimensions of the original.

⑤ Click **Compose**.

iPhoto tells Mail or your designated email application to create a new email message and attaches the selected image to the message.

6 Type a recipient email address.

Note: To look up email addresses in Address Book, see Chapter 4.

● Type a subject description for the message.

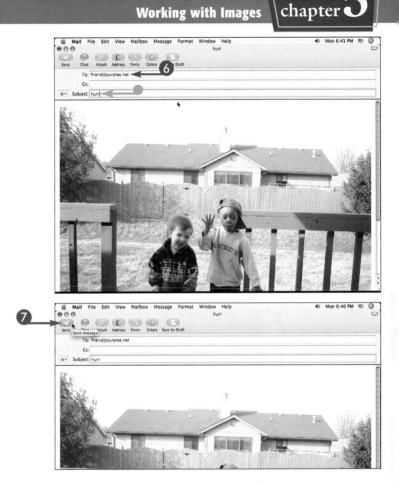

7 Click the **Send** button.

Mail sends the message.

TIPS

Will my friend with Microsoft Windows be able to read the email messages created from iPhoto?

Email messages are universally compatible, so long as you click the **Windows Friendly Attachments** checkbox in the Mail's Open sheet. Windows users should have no problems seeing images that you send from iPhoto.

Can I email multiple images in the same email?

Yes. To email multiple images, follow the steps in this task, but in step 2, ⌘ +click the images that you want to send before clicking the Email button in step 3. Keep in mind that AOL users can run into trouble if you attach more than one image to an email message.

You can view the images in
your iPhoto Library as a
slideshow. iPhoto automates
the process and plays your
collection in full-screen format.
You can stop and start the
slideshow, as well as control its
progress, using the keyboard.

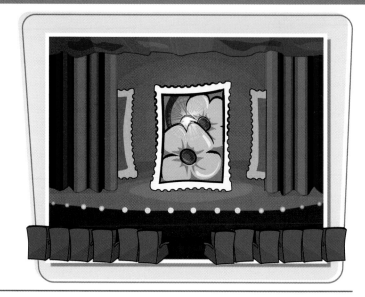

Watch a Slideshow

① In iPhoto, click a Photo Album that you want to view.

You can click the **Library** if you want to view the
entire photo collection.

iPhoto displays the photo tools.

② To begin viewing a slideshow, click **Slideshow**.

A Slideshow settings window appears.

③ Click and select a transition effect to show between photos.

The Cube transition rotates between two images as if they were drawn on two sides of a cube.

④ Click **Music**.

⑤ Click a song to play during the slideshow.

⑥ Click **OK**.

⑦ Click **Play**.

The screen fades to black and the slideshow begins playing.

Do I have to sit and wait through each photo in the slideshow?

The ← and → keys are still active during the slideshow. To skip a photo, press the →. To return to the previous image in the slideshow, press ←.

How do I stop a slideshow from playing?

Press Esc to stop a playing slideshow. The iPhoto interface returns to the foreground. You can also pause the video of a slideshow by pressing the Spacebar. Press Spacebar again to resume slideshow playback.

Print a Picture Using iPhoto

iPhoto does a great job of displaying beautiful images on your monitor, but sometimes you want a copy of an image. You can print your images with iPhoto, too.

① In iPhoto, click **Library**.

② Click an image in the Photo Library.

If you want to print on a paper size other than 8.5" x 11", click **File,** then click **Page Setup** and adjust the page settings.

③ Click the **Print** button.

The print dialog box appears.

④ Click ⬍ and select a printer.

⑤ Click ⬍ and select a preset.

⑥ Click ⬍ and select a style.

Style allows you to print on one of several different layouts, including a full page and greeting cards.

⑦ Click **Preview**.

Preview launches.

8 If you are satisfied with the way the preview looks, click **Print**.

Click **Cancel** if you want to change the page setup.

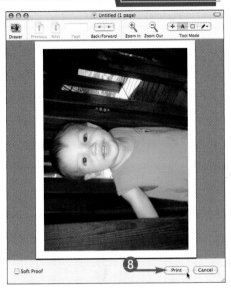

Preview prints the photo.

Why do I have to launch Preview to print an iPhoto image?

iPhoto uses Preview strictly for displaying a preview of the print job. If you do not feel compelled to see the preview of the iPhoto print job, you can click the **Print** button to print directly to a printer.

How do I save print dialog settings for later use?

Each print dialog box has a **Presets** popup menu. In that popup menu, click **Save As** to create a new preset that represents the current print settings. Later, when you want to reuse the preset, select it from the list of choices in the **Presets** pop-up menu.

CHAPTER 6

Listening to Music

Mac OS X comes stocked with everything you need to listen to and manipulate music. This chapter introduces you to Tiger's music tools and shows you how to import and play music, tweak the audio to your liking, organize songs into a collection, create a playlist, burn a CD, and print a case insert for the CD. You can also listen to online radio and share your music with others over a network.

Listen to Music with QuickTime Player

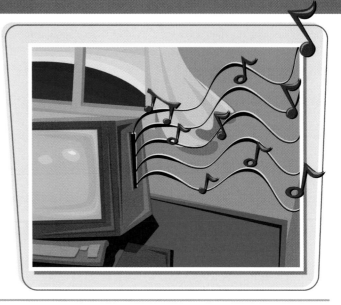

QuickTime Player is a multipurpose multimedia powerhouse. With it, you can play audio in a variety of formats. You can use QuickTime Player to listen to MP3 music files from your collection, audio files that you download from the Internet, or songs that you create with GarageBand. You can also control playback in QuickTime Player with the keyboard.

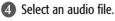

Listen to Music with QuickTime Player

① Click **QuickTime Player**.

The QuickTime Player application launches.

② Click **File**.

③ Click **Open Movie**.

An Open dialog box appears where you can choose a media file to open.

④ Select an audio file.

⑤ Click **Open**.

QuickTime Player opens the audio file in its own player window.

6 Click **Play** () changes to (▣).

You can also press the space bar to play the file.

The audio file begins playing.

To stop playback, click (▣).

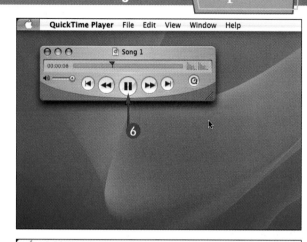

● You can drag ⊙ left to lower the volume or right to increase the volume.

Click (◄) to locate the beginning of the song or (►) to find the end of the song.

● You can click and drag the playhead (▼) to a specific point in the song.

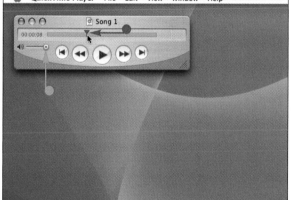

TIPS

What types of audio files can QuickTime Player play?

QuickTime Player can play a large number of audio file formats. The most common formats that you might encounter are AIFF, WAV, MP3, and M4P. AIFF files, like those that GarageBand produces, are usually in a high quality, uncompressed format. WAV files are common on the Microsoft Windows and are analogous to AIFF. MP3 and M4P are compressed file formats. They provide reduced fidelity compared to uncompressed AIFF or WAV, but the file size is very small in comparison. Because of their reduced size, MP3 and M4P formats are in common use on iPods and in iTunes.

How do I use the keyboard to control QuickTime Player?

Open an audio file in QuickTime Player. Press **Space** to begin playback. Press **Space** again to stop playback. Press ⌘ + ⬆ to increase the volume. Press ⌘ + ⬇ to decrease the volume.

Listen to Music in the Finder

You do not need a special application to listen to music with your Macintosh. Tiger provides preview playback of many common audio formats directly in the Finder. The audio quality is the same as in an audio application and the Finder allows you to quickly listen to a file without having to launch an audio application.

Listen to Music in the Finder

PREVIEW AN AUDIO FILE

1. In the Finder, locate and click an MP3 file.

2. Click **File**.

3. Click **Get Info**.

   An Info window opens for that file.

4. Click the **Preview** triangle (▶).

PLAY THE AUDIO FILE

A small player appears in Preview.

⑤ Click **Play** (▶ changes to ❚❚).

The audio file begins playing.

● To adjust the volume, click ◀ᐧ and drag the slider up or down.

```
○ ○ ○        Song 1.mp3 Info
```

Song 1.mp3   452 KB
Modified: Aug 11, 2004 1:47 AM

▶ Spotlight Comments:

▼ General:

Kind: MP3 Audio File
Size: 452 KB on disk (459,431 bytes)
Where: /Users/e/Music/Music
Created: Friday, January 12, 2001 3:26 AM
Modified: Wednesday, August 11, 2004 1:47 AM

Color label: ✗ ● ● ● ● ● ● ●

☐ Stationery Pad
☐ Locked

▶ More Info:
▶ Name & Extension:
▶ Open with:
▼ Preview:

◀ᐧ ▶ ○———— ◀❙ ❙▶

▶ Ownership & Permissions:

⑤

```
○ ○ ○        Song 1.mp3 Info
```

▼ General:

Song 1.mp3

Kind: MP3 Audio File
Size: 452 KB on disk (459,431 bytes)
Where: /Users/e/Music/Music
Created: Friday, January 12, 2001 3:26 AM
Modified: Wednesday, August 11, 2004 1:47 AM

Color label: ✗ ● ● ● ● ● ● ●
☐ Stationery Pad
☐ Locked

▶ More Info:
▶ Name & Extension:
▶ Open with:
▼ Preview:

◀ᐧ ❚❚ ——○————— ◀❙ ❙▶

▶ Ownership & Permissions:
▶ Comments:

TIPS

What audio file formats can I preview in the Finder?

You can preview any file format that QuickTime will play. For audio files, this includes many common audio formats like MP3, AIFF, WAV, and AAC. QuickTime treats all of these formats similarly, displaying an audio player in the Finder window when you select a file. The Finder does not display a preview player for any file types that QuickTime does not understand.

What hidden features are in the Preview section of the Info window?

Thanks to universal QuickTime support, the Preview section of an Info window has many of the same features that other QuickTime applications do. You can Shift +click the volume slider to increase the volume beyond 100 percent. You can also use the "scrub" controls by Control +clicking either the Rewind or Forward buttons on the player.

Listen to Music with iTunes

iTunes is the premiere music player in Mac OS X Tiger. You can use iTunes to listen to a song, a whole list of songs, or random songs in the iTunes Library. iTunes functions like a CD player in that you can advance and retreat in a playlist and repeat songs or entire playlists that you like.

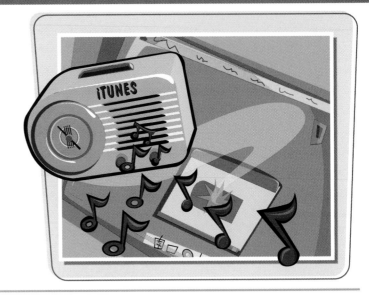

Listen to Music with iTunes

PLAY A SONG

① Click **iTunes**.

The iTunes application launches.

② Click **Library**.

iTunes displays all songs in the Library.

③ Double-click a song.

The song begins playing.

You can also play a song by selecting it and pressing the space bar.

④ Click Pause (𝗜𝗜).

You can also press the Spacebar.

The song stops playing.

ADVANCE TO THE NEXT SONG

⑤ Click ▶ .

The song you selected in the Library begins playing.

⑥ Click **Next** (⏭) or press ➡ .

The next song in the Library plays.

PLAY THE PREVIOUS SONG

⑦ Click ▶.

The song you selected in the Library begins playing.

⑧ Click **Previous** (◀◀) or press ◀ .

The previous song in the Library plays.

REPEAT A SONG

⑨ Click ▶.

The song you selected in the Library begins playing.

⑩ Click **Repeat** (↻).

iTunes continues playing each song and will repeat the entire Library once it finishes playing.

⑪ Click ↻ again.

iTunes repeats the current song until you either stop playback or deactivate repeat.

⑫ Click ↻ a third time.

iTunes deactivates repeat playback.

TIPS

How do I cause iTunes to play songs randomly?

In the Source list, click **Party Shuffle**. iTunes displays a playlist composed of random selections from the Library. If you do not like the selection of random songs, click the **Refresh** button in the upper-right corner of the iTunes window to create a new random list of songs.

I forget which Repeat button icon is which. Is there another way to toggle the repeat modes?

You can toggle the repeat modes by clicking the appropriate submenu in the **Controls** menu. The **Repeat One** menu repeats one song multiple times. The **Repeat All** menu item plays all songs in the current playlist of Library and then repeats them.

Import CD Audio in iTunes

iTunes gives you relief from constantly switching CDs. You can import audio from any audio CD and have it instantly accessible without ever needing the disc again. iTunes stores the songs on your hard drive. You can adjust the quality of iTunes imports to manage the size of files.

Import CD Audio in iTunes

① Put a music CD in your Macintosh.

● iTunes launches and the CD appears in the iTunes Source List.

If you have not played this CD before, iTunes retrieves the song titles and disc information for you from the Internet.

② Click **iTunes**.

③ Click **Preferences**.

The Preferences sheet opens.

④ Click Importing.

The Preferences sheet displays import settings.

⑤ Click ⊡ and select an encoder.

⑥ Click ⊡ and select a quality setting.

These settings tell iTunes to import audio files as high-quality MP3 files.

⑦ Click **OK**.

The Preferences sheet closes.

⑧ Click the CD in the Source list to make it active.

⑨ Click **Import** (⊡).

iTunes begins importing songs on the CD.

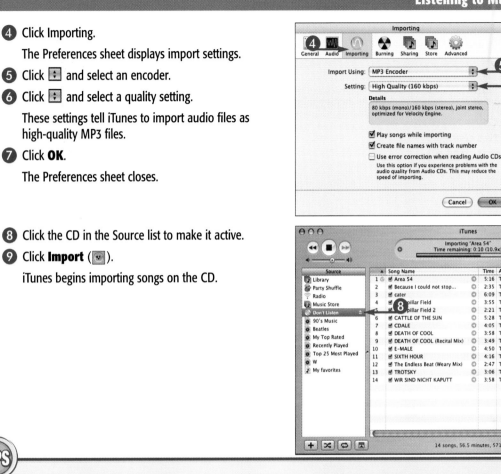

Why does the CD begin playing automatically when I import songs from a CD?

iTunes has a default preference that causes CDs to automatically begin playback. The Importing Preferences has a checkbox that you can use to toggle this setting. When unchecked, the CD will not play when you initiate an import.

Where are the songs stored after I import them?

In iTunes, the imported songs appear in the Library. In the Finder, the song files appear in your Home folder in ~/Music/iTunes/iTunes Music/ArtistName/ AlbumName/. Songs in your iTunes library can also reside elsewhere on your hard drive. To prevent iTunes from copying imported files to the iTunes folder in your Music folder, uncheck the **Copy files to iTunes Music folder when adding to library** checkbox in the **Advanced** pane of the preferences window.

Organize a Music Collection

You can organize your music according to many different criteria to help you find your favorite songs quickly. You can find songs in the your iTunes Library by searching for particular song attributes, such as artist, album title, composer, and year. This rapidly accelerates your ability to locate music in your collection.

Organize a Music Collection

SWITCH VIEWS

① In iTunes, click **Library**.

② Click **Browse**.

The iTunes interface displays columns like Artist and Album to help you organize your music.

③ Click **Browse** again.

The iTunes interface hides the organizational columns and displays the library as one long list.

SELECT COLUMNS TO VIEW

4️⃣ Press ⌘ + J .

The View Options window appears.

5️⃣ Click the column you want to display
(☐ changes to ☑).

In this example, the Play Count column is selected.

6️⃣ Click **OK**.

The View Options window closes.

7️⃣ Click a column name.

When clicking **Play Count**, iTunes sorts the songs according to the number of times you have played them.

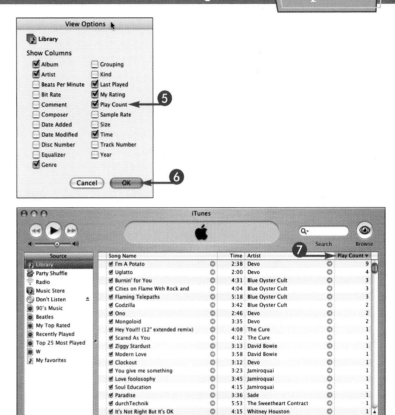

What does the small triangle at the top of a column header mean?

The small triangle at the top of the currently selected column header indicates the order by which iTunes sorts. When the arrow points up, the sort order is alphabetical for text or smallest to largest for numbers. When the arrow points down, iTunes sorts in reverse alphabetical for text and largest to smallest for numerical columns.

The Album column is too narrow to read the names of some albums. How can I correct this?

You can resize any column by clicking and dragging the vertical line on the right side of each column heading. You can reduce the number of columns displayed in the Library by changing settings in the View Options window. Open the View Options window by clicking **View Options** in the **Edit** menu.

Build a Playlist

You can organize your music into playlists for one-click access to your collection. After you create a playlist, you can add songs to and delete songs from it. To keep the music interesting, you can shuffle songs in a playlist.

CREATE A NEW PLAYLIST

1 Click ⊞.

A new playlist appears in the Source list.

2 Type a name for the playlist.

3 Press Return.

iTunes renames the new playlist.

ADD A SONG TO A PLAYLIST

1 Click **Library**.

2 Drag a song from the Library onto a playlist's icon.

iTunes adds the song to the playlist.

REMOVE A SONG FROM A PLAYLIST

1 Click a playlist icon.

The playlist appears.

2 Click a song icon in the playlist to select it.

3 Press Delete .

iTunes removes the song from the playlist.

SHUFFLE SONGS IN A PLAYLIST

1 Click Shuffle ⚇.

iTunes shuffles the order of songs in the playlist.

2 Click ⚇ again.

The playlist returns to its original order.

TIP

If I delete a song from a playlist, is it also gone from my Library and erased from my hard drive?

No. The songs in a playlist are just pointers to the songs in the Library. If you delete a song in a playlist, the song remains in the Library. If you delete a song from the Library, however, you cannot add the song to a playlist until you import it again. When you remove a song from the Library or a playlist, iTunes does not delete the song from your hard drive. Instead, iTunes asks if you want to move the file to the Trash or leave it in its current location in the Finder.

Create a
Smart Playlist

You can organize your music
dynamically into a group called a
Smart Playlist. A Smart Playlist is
a collection of songs that have
one or more features in common.
One of the most popular uses for
Smart Playlists is to display a list
of music by a particular artist. As
you add new songs to the Library,
they appear in any Smart Playlists
that pertain to them.

Create a Smart Playlist

① Click **File**.

② Click **New Smart Playlist**.

The Smart Playlist dialog box appears.

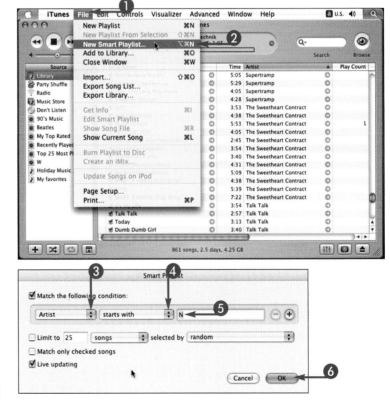

③ Click 🔽 and select a parameter.

This example selects **Artist**.

④ Click 🔽 and select a search rule.

This example selects **starts with**.

⑤ Type a letter in the field.

This example displays the letter **N**.

⑥ Click **OK**.

A new Smart Playlist appears, displaying all songs
where the Artist's name begins with the letter N.

ASSIGN ADDITIONAL SEARCH CRITERIA

7 Click ⊕.

8 Click ◆ and select a parameter (**Genre** in this example).

9 Click ◆ and select a search rule (**contains** in this example).

10 Type a keyword (the genre **Rock** in this example).

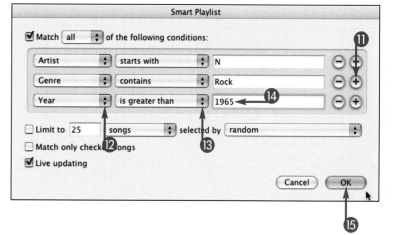

11 Click ⊕.

iTunes adds a new rule to the Smart Playlist.

12 Click ◆ and select a parameter (**Year** in this example).

13 Click ◆ and select a search rule (**is greater than** in this example).

14 Type **1965**.

15 Click **OK**.

iTunes adds a Smart Playlist that displays all Rock songs from the library that begin with N and that were recorded after 1965.

TIPS

If I add songs to the Library later, will I have to update my Smart Playlists?

Because Smart Playlists are generated dynamically, you do not need to update Smart Playlists when you import new songs. iTunes reapplies your parameters to determine which songs belong in each Smart Playlist.

If I add songs to the Library later, will I have to update my Playlists?

Standard Playlists do not share the same dynamic capabilities that Smart Playlists do. You must update Playlists if you want them to include new music that you have added to the Library. Likewise, if you remove an audio file from your hard drive, you will also have to remove it from any Playlist that contains it.

You can burn a music CD in iTunes that is playable in most CD music players and a large number of DVD players. Burning CDs is useful for organizing your favorite music into unique collections or for making backups of your music collection.

Burn a Music CD

SELECT A PLAYLIST

1. Click a playlist in the iTunes Source list to select it.

   iTunes will use the order and song selections in this playlist to create a new audio CD.

2. Click the first column header.

3. Rearrange the song order by clicking and dragging a song to the desired position in the list.

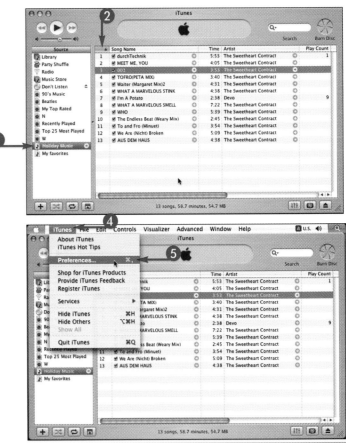

SELECT THE AUDIO CD FORMAT

4. Click **iTunes**.

5. Click **Preferences**.

   The Preferences window opens.

6 Click **Burning**.

7 Click the **Audio CD** option (○ changes to ●).

8 Click **OK**.

The Preferences window closes.

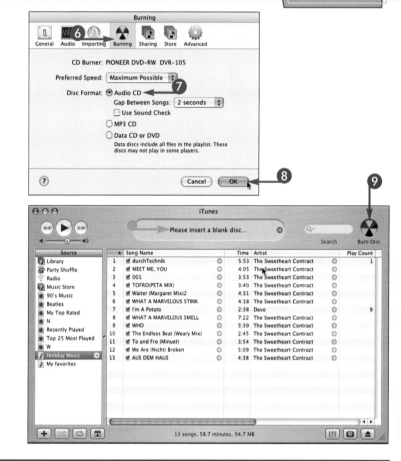

BURN THE CD

9 Click **Burn Disc**.

iTunes requests a blank CD.

10 Insert a blank CD and click **Burn Disc** again.

iTunes proceeds to burn the CD.

TIPS

How much music can an audio CD hold?

A typical 650MB CD can store approximately 74 minutes of music, and the typical 700MB CD can store approximately 80 minutes of CD-quality audio. If you choose MP3 instead, you can store many more songs on one CD. The MP3 compression permits the storage capacity to jump to over eight hours of music. Only some CD players recognize MP3 CDs, but most DVD players do.

How can I adjust the levels of all songs so that they match each other during playback?

iTunes has a feature called Sound Check that automatically adjusts volume levels so that every track plays at a similar volume. To activate Sound Check, open the iTunes preferences window and click the **Audio** button in the preferences window toolbar. Finally, click the **Sound Check** check box to activate it.

Print a CD Case Insert

You can print a CD cover directly from iTunes. The cover can display artwork as well as playlist information like song titles and artist names. Besides CD case inserts, you can print a list of your entire iTunes Library or save it as a PDF file.

ADD ARTWORK TO SONGS

① Click a playlist to select it.

iTunes uses the order of songs in this playlist to create a CD cover.

② Click a song in the playlist.

③ Click **Artwork** (⬛).

iTunes displays the song's artwork. If no artwork is present, a gray outline appears with the words "Drag Album Artwork Here."

④ To add or change artwork, click and drag an image file from the Finder and drop it onto the Artwork section.

PRINT THE INSERT

1 Click **File**.

2 Click **Print**.

The Print dialog box appears.

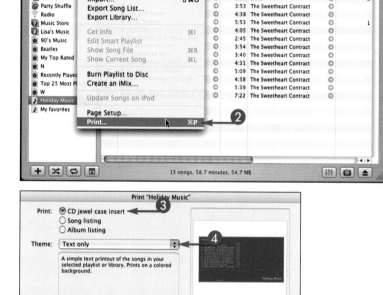

3 Click the **CD jewel case insert** option
(○ changes to ●).

4 Click 🔽 and select **Text only**.

5 Click **Print**.

The print job consists of a cover for a CD jewel case with the playlist title on the front and song titles on the back.

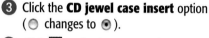
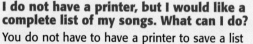

TIPS

What other types of printing can I do with iTunes?

In addition to CD jewel cases, you can print a complete list of songs or albums in a Playlist or the Library. To do so, select **Print** from the **File** menu. In the Print dialog, click **Album Listing**, which will print a list of all albums in the currently selected Playlist or Library. Finally, click the **Print** button.

I do not have a printer, but I would like a complete list of my songs. What can I do?

You do not have to have a printer to save a list of your iTunes collection. To save the output of a print job to a file, click Save as PDF in the standard print dialog. You can use the PDF file later to print from another computer that has a printer attached. You can attach the PDF to an email message to share your song list with friends too. A PDF file is also a good tool for itemizing your possessions for things like insurance.

Share Music on the Network

To expand your listening opportunities, you can listen to music that is stored in other iTunes libraries on the local network. Likewise, other listeners on the network can listen to music in your iTunes library. To prevent others from overusing your resources, you can limit sharing to specific playlists in your Library.

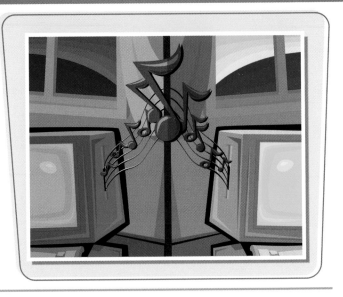

LET OTHERS LISTEN TO YOUR MUSIC

① Click **iTunes**.

② Click **Preferences**.

The iTunes Preferences window opens.

③ Click **Sharing**.

The Sharing settings appear.

④ Click **Share my music** (☑ changes to ☐).

⑤ Click **Share entire library** (◯ changes to ◉).

⑥ Click **OK** to close the Preferences window.

Other users can now browse and listen to music in your library.

If a user attempts to play a protected song, iTunes requires the user to be authorized.

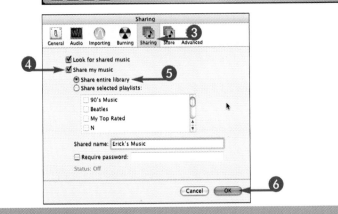

LISTEN TO MUSIC ON THE NETWORK

1 Click a Shared Playlist.

A Shared Playlist icon () appears in the Sidebar for each user that is sharing on the local network.

● When you click , iTunes displays the shared songs from that user's computer.

2 Click a song.

3 Click ▶.

iTunes begins playing the song.

TIPS

Can someone outside my office or home listen to my music?

The sharing feature in iTunes is only for use within a local area network. No one outside of the local network can access your music. If you click **Require password** in Preferences, you can restrict access to users on the local network. Music that you purchase from the iTunes store is also protected so that only authorized people can listen to it.

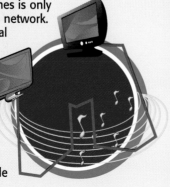

Can more than one person at a time listen to my music?

iTunes will gladly share music with multiple users at once, all playing different songs or the same song. All users on the network will be able to listen to the playlists or Library on your machine. To permit only certain users to have access, you can password-protect your computer in the Sharing pane of the iTunes Preferences window.

Adjust the Sound Quality of iTunes

You can adjust the sound that iTunes produces by adjusting the equalizer and editing the audio preferences. The equalizer helps you mold the sound of a song by boosting or cutting frequencies. With the equalizer, you can accentuate weak bass in a song or remove unwanted hiss from live recordings. iTunes can also automatically fade in at the beginning of a song or fade out at the end.

SET THE EQUALIZER FOR AN IDEAL SOUND

1 In iTunes, click Equalizer (⊞).

The equalizer window opens.

2 Click ⬍ and select an equalizer setting.

The equalizer changes the frequency sliders to settings that are appropriate for the music style that you selected.

This example selects the Electronic equalizer setting.

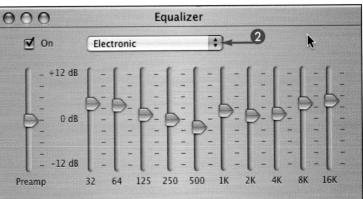

3 Click and drag one of the sliders to a new setting.

This example adjusts the **2K** slider to make vocals stand out.

● The drop-down menu changes to Manual, indicating that you are no longer using an equalizer preset.

4 Click ⊙ to close the equalizer.

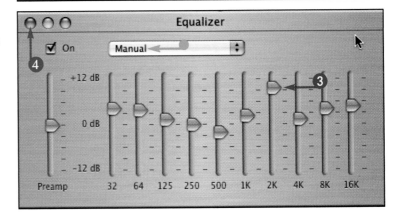

SET AUDIO PREFERENCES

1 Click **iTunes**.

2 Click **Preferences**.

The iTunes Preferences window opens.

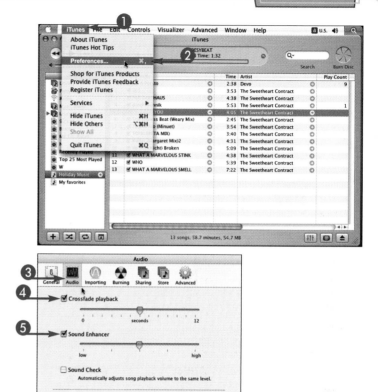

3 Click **Audio**.

The Audio preferences appear.

4 Click **Crossfade playback** (☐ changes to ☑).

This setting enables music to fade in at the beginning of a song and out at the end.

5 Click **Sound Enhancer** (☐ changes to ☑).

This setting processes the audio to make it sound brighter with more presence, but if you set it too high, the audio can sound harsh and distorted.

TIPS

What does the Sound Check option do?

Selecting the Sound Check option in Audio Preferences causes iTunes to automatically adjust the volume of each track so that the overall volume remains constant.

I see AirTunes mentioned in the Audio Preferences. What is that?

AirTunes is a protocol by which iTunes can talk to an AirPort Express device. An AirPort Express can play iTunes music wirelessly through a traditional stereo.

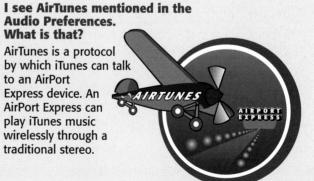

Watch Visual Effects While Listening

You can run a visual light show on your screen while iTunes is playing music. It plays soothing animations and helps hide your work while you are away from the computer. iTunes has a collection of different visuals from which you can choose. You can also change the screen settings for the visuals.

Watch Visual Effects While Listening

ADJUST VISUALIZER SETTINGS

① Click **Visualizer**.

② Click **Large**.

With this setting, iTunes draws the graphics in a large rectangle within the iTunes window.

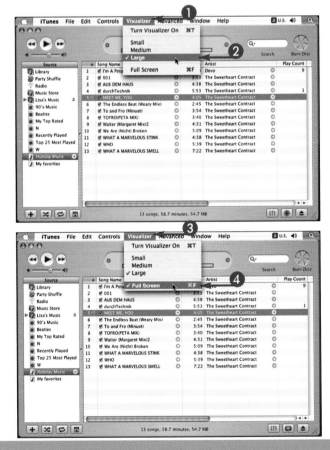

③ Click **Visualizer**.

④ Click **Full Screen**.

This setting causes iTunes to darken everything on the screen, including the menu bar before displaying animations.

DISPLAY THE VISUALIZER

1 Click **Visualizer**.

2 Click **Turn Visualizer On**.

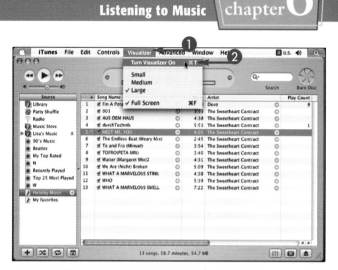

iTunes blackens the screen and begins playing a graphics animation.

3 Click the mouse.

iTunes stops the animation and displays the regular interface.

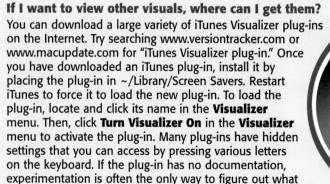

If I want to view other visuals, where can I get them?

You can download a large variety of iTunes Visualizer plug-ins on the Internet. Try searching www.versiontracker.com or www.macupdate.com for "iTunes Visualizer plug-in." Once you have downloaded an iTunes plug-in, install it by placing the plug-in in ~/Library/Screen Savers. Restart iTunes to force it to load the new plug-in. To load the plug-in, locate and click its name in the **Visualizer** menu. Then, click **Turn Visualizer On** in the **Visualizer** menu to activate the plug-in. Many plug-ins have hidden settings that you can access by pressing various letters on the keyboard. If the plug-in has no documentation, experimentation is often the only way to figure out what settings the plug-in has.

Listen to Online Radio Stations

In addition to the selections in your iTunes Library, you can listen to online radio stations. Radio stations around the world broadcast Internet streams that you can hear using iTunes. You can locate and save radio stations that you enjoy listening to, so that you can easily access them later, much as you would create and save Playlists. In fact, radio stations can coexist with MP3 files in playlists.

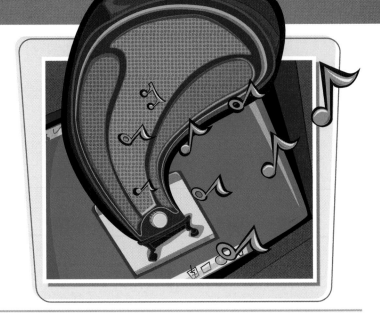

LOCATE RADIO STATIONS

① In the iTunes Source list, click **Radio**.

● iTunes displays a list of radio categories.

② Double-click a category.

iTunes shows the radio stations available in that category.

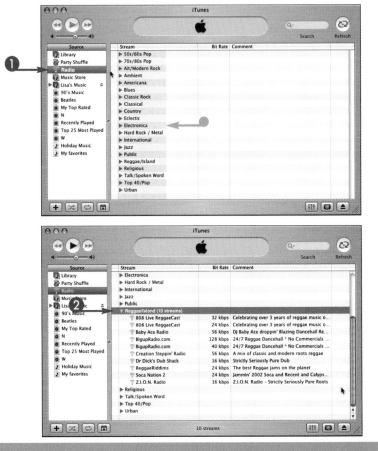

LISTEN TO A STATION

③ Double-click a radio station.

iTunes downloads the stream for the radio station and begins playing it.

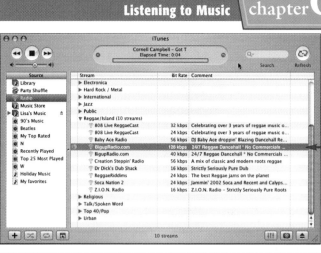

SAVE A STATION

① Click and drag a radio station from the Radio list to an existing playlist.

② Click the playlist in the Sidebar.

The Radio station appears in the playlist.

TIPS

Can I add my own radio stations that I find on the Internet?

You can create your own radio station entries in a playlist. Create a new entry by clicking and dragging an existing radio station to a playlist. Then, press ⌘ + I to open the Info window for the station, where you can paste in a different URL for a new radio station that you want to save.

How fast must my connection be to listen to radio stations on the Internet?

As with most things that involve a network, the faster your network, the better your results. In general this means that you will want a broadband Internet connection for optimal results. Modem users can still enjoy Internet radio, though, since many stations offer slower streams that modems can use without skipping or other listening degradations.

Watching and Editing Video

Mac OS X Tiger turns your Mac into a movie theater and production house. With Tiger, you can watch video files and DVDs much like you would watch a television. You can also create your own movies with iMovie by capturing clips from a video camera, editing the footage, and sharing the results.

Watch Movies with QuickTime Player

QuickTime Player is a multipurpose multimedia player. You can use it watch movie files in a multitude of formats. You can customize the QuickTime Player during playback by resizing a movie window. You can also adjust the sound during playback.

Watch Movies with QuickTime Player

PLAY A MOVIE FILE

① In the Dock, click **QuickTime Player**.

The QuickTime Player application launches.

② Click **File**.

③ Click **Open File**.

An Open dialog box appears where you can choose a movie file to open.

④ Select a movie file.

⑤ Click **Open**.

QuickTime Player opens the movie file in its own player window.

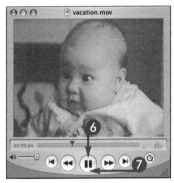

⑥ Click the Play button (▶) or press the space bar.

The movie file begins playing (▶ changes to ⏸).

⑦ Click ⏸ or press the space bar again.

The movie stops playing.

TIPS

What types of movie files can QuickTime Player play?

QuickTime Player can play many different movie file formats. The most common formats are MOV, DV, and MPEG-4. To a limited degree, QuickTime can play AVI format too. QuickTime relies on codec plug-ins to play and convert varying video formats. If a plug-in is not available for a particular video format, QuickTime cannot play or convert it.

How do I adjust the sound and change the screen size of a movie?

You can adjust the volume of a QuickTime movie by moving its Volume slider. You can also increase the volume by pressing ⌘+↑ and ⌘+↓ to decrease the volume. To change the size of a movie window, click and drag the bottom right corner of the movie window. To constrain the movie's dimensions to its original size, press and hold Shift while you resize the window.

Watch Movies in DVD Player

If your Mac has a DVD-compatible drive, you can watch a movie from a standard DVD using DVD Player. You can resize the DVD Player window to fit on your desktop while you work. To control the playback of DVD Player, you can use the floating control panel. There, you can play, stop, and navigate the menu for the DVD.

LAUNCH DVD PLAYER AND BEGIN PLAYBACK

① Insert a DVD into your Macintosh.

The Mac launches DVD Player and the DVD begins playing automatically.

Note: The DVD in this example displays a menu. The disc you insert may behave differently.

After a short pause, DVD Player displays a floating control panel.

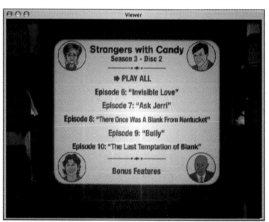

STOP THE MOVIE

② Click **Stop** (⊙).

The movie stops playing and the DVD Player window turns black.

RETURN TO THE MAIN MENU

③ Click **Menu**.

If the DVD has a menu, it appears on the screen.

ADJUST THE SIZE OF MOVIE PLAYBACK

④ Click **Video**.

⑤ Click **Half Size, Normal Size, Maximum Size,** or **Enter Full Screen**.

The movie window resizes to the selected size.

TIPS

When the DVD Player is playing in full-screen mode the menu bar is hidden during playback. How do I click the menu bar?

Move the mouse to the top of the screen to make the menu bar reappear. You can also press Esc to make the menu bar appear. After you have finished making menu selections, stop using the mouse and the keyboard. After a brief pause, the menu bar once again disappears, giving you full-screen playback.

What options usually appear in DVD menus?

DVD menus usually give you some control over playback of the video. Often, menus contain settings for changing the language spoken in the soundtrack. You may also find subtitle options in the menu. The menu often gives you access to the various chapters in the movie, so you can skip ahead to important scenes in the video.

Capture Clips from a Camcorder

You can import video directly from a FireWire camera into iMovie. You can also remotely control most digital camcorders from iMovie. As you capture various clips from a camcorder, you can store the clips in your iMovie project.

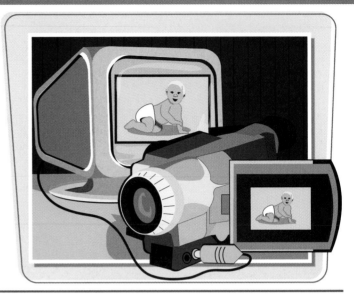

SET IMOVIE TO CAMERA MODE

1 Connect a FireWire cable to a video camera and to a Mac.

iMovie does not automatically detect the camcorder until it is powered on.

2 Turn on the camcorder.

3 In iMovie, click ▣.

● iMovie switches to camera mode.

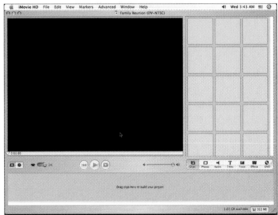

④ Click ▶.

Video from the camera begins playing in the iMovie Monitor.

⑤ Once you find video that you want to import from the camera, click **Import** .

iMovie begins capturing video from the camera.

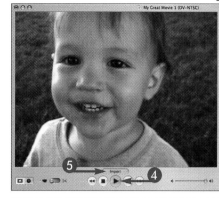

⑥ Click **Import** again.

● iMovie stops capturing video and places the clips in the **Clips** pane.

⑦ Click **Stop** (■).

iMovie stops capturing video from the video camera.

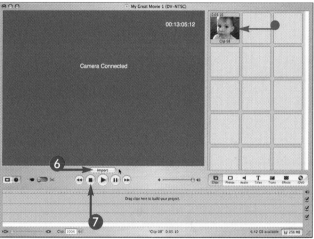

 TIPS

Can I control other aspects of video camera operation from the iMovie HD interface?

You can rewind, fast-forward, play, pause, and stop a video camera from the iMovie HD interface. The tape control buttons in the main iMovie HD interface control cameras when iMovie HD is in camera mode. Clicking these control buttons is analogous to pressing the buttons on the camera itself.

Why do multiple clips appear in the Clips pane when I capture footage from my video camcorder?

iMovie HD breaks up clips captured from your camcorder automatically at scene breaks and 12GB intervals (about one hour). It detects the places on your videotape where you stopped and started recording and makes those the start and endpoints or captured clips. As you import footage, the different clips appear in the Clips pane.

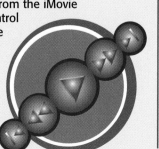

You can import video clips from different sources to use in the movies you create in iMovie HD. After you import a video clip, you can preview it before adding it to the movie timeline.

Import Video Clips

1. In iMovie HD, click **File**.

2. Click **Import**.

   The Open sheet appears.

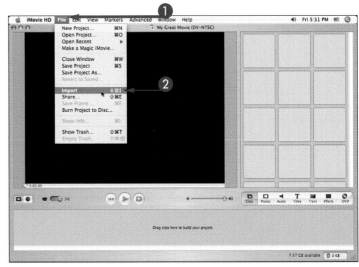

3. Click a video file to import.

4. Click **Open**.

   iMovie imports the movie and places it in the Clips section of the interface.

● You can click **Cancel** if you want to stop the import operation before has completed.

PREVIEW A CLIP

⑤ Click **Clips**.

The clips for this project appear in the Clips pane.

⑥ Click a clip that you want to preview.

⑦ Click **Play** (▶).

The clip begins playing (▶ changes to ⏸).

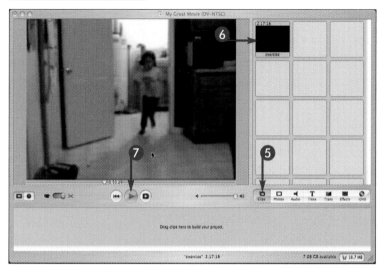

TIPS

iMovie will not import my movie file. What can I do about this?

iMovie will only permit the import of certain file types. One such format is MOV. You can convert some movie formats like MP4 and some AVI files to MOV format with QuickTime Player. Other movie formats, like MPEG-1 or MPEG-2, lose audio when you perform a conversion to MOV. Further, QuickTime Pro is required to convert movie files to MOV. You can also perform file conversions with free utilities like MPEG Streamclip, available at www. alfanet.it/squared5/ mpegstreamclip.html.

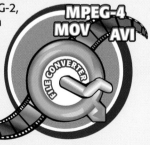

iMovie HD said that my imported clip is too large. What is the largest file I can import?

Versions of iMovie prior to version iMovie HD permit you to import files as large as 2GB. iMovie HD removes this limit and increases it to 12GB. If you exceed the maximum clip size, you can get around the problem by importing multiple smaller clips.

Add Clips to the Movie Timeline

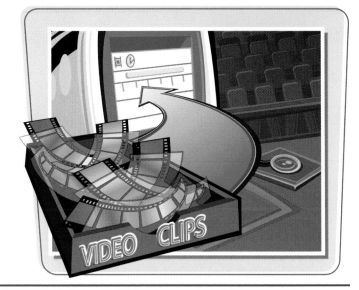

To construct a movie, you can add video clips to the Timeline. You can reorder the clips in the Timeline to edit the movie. You can also edit individual clips before you add them to the Timeline. Editing functions include changing the length of a clip and its position in the Timeline.

Add Clips to the Movie Timeline

DRAG CLIPS TO THE TIMELINE

① Drag and drop a clip from the Clips pane to the Timeline.

The clip appears in the Timeline.

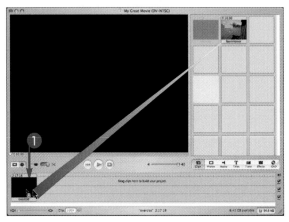

② Drag a second clip to the Timeline.

The clip appears in the Timeline to the right of the first clip.

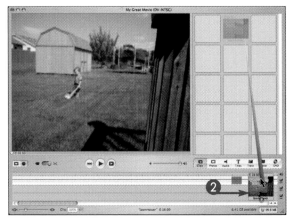

EDIT CLIPS

③ Click and drag the first clip, dropping it behind the second clip.

The second clip moves over into the place of the first clip, which is now the second clip in the Timeline.

④ To cut off the end of a clip, click 🕒 to switch to the **Timeline viewer.**

This is a non-destructive edit, since it does not destroy the original movie.

⑤ Move the cursor over the end of the clip in the Timeline.

🖰 changes to 🖰 to indicate that you can make an edit.

⑥ Click and drag the right edge of the clip to the left.

The clip gets shorter as you drag it to the left.

TIPS

Can I also change the starting point of the video?

You can edit the beginning of a movie in the same manner that you edit the end. Move the cursor to the beginning of the clip and click. As you drag, the video begins playing later in the clip. If you make a mistake and remove too much of the clip, you can edit the clip again.

How can I play a clip in reverse?

You can play a clip in reverse by Control -clicking a clip in the Timeline. A contextual menu opens revealing the Reverse Clip Direction option. Click that option to reverse the clip. Later, if you decide that you do not like the reversed clip, simply reverse it again to return it to its original forward state.

Add Photos to the Movie Timeline

You can add photos to movies to play back in a slideshow. You can also add motion, called the Ken Burns effects, to still photos to give the video a professional appearance. After you apply the Ken Burns effect to a clip, you can continue to edit the effect and update the clip.

Add Photos to the Movie Timeline

DRAG PHOTOS TO THE TIMELINE

① In iMovie HD, click **Photos**.

iMovie displays the photographs in your iPhoto Library.

② Click and drag a photo to the Timeline.

The photo appears in the Timeline.

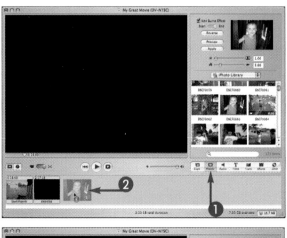

ZOOM IN ON A PHOTO IN IMOVIE

① Click a photo.

② Click and drag 🔘 to adjust the size.

The photo preview zooms in when you move to the right and out when you move to the left.

③ Click **Update**.

The resized photo appears in the Timeline.

ADD THE KEN BURNS EFFECT

1 Click a photo.

2 Click **Ken Burns Effect** (☐ changes to ☑).

3 Click **Preview**.

The effect plays in the preview window.

The size slider displays the size of the photo at the beginning of the Ken Burns Effect clip.

4 Click **End.**

The size slider displays the size of the photo at the end of the Ken Burns Effect clip.

5 Click **Update**.

The clip with the Ken Burns Effect applied appears in the Timeline.

TIPS

How do I edit an existing Ken Burns Effect in the Timeline?

Click the clip in the Timeline. The Apply button in the Photos panel turns into an Update button. Move the **Start** and **Finish** sliders to modify the zoom of the clip at the beginning and end of the Ken Burns Effect. Then, click **Update** to update the clip with the new settings.

Who is Ken Burns and why is there an effect named after him?

Ken Burns is a world-renowned documentarian. Because his documentaries often display many still photographs to tell a story, he came up with the idea to add a subtle panning or zooming effect to a still image. This gives photos a movie-like quality and makes them somewhat more interesting to watch.

Mix Audio in the Soundtrack

You can add music, sound effects, and narration to a movie. Music helps define the mood of a movie, sound effects add realism, and narration gives the viewer important information. The iMovie Timeline has two audio tracks where you can add audio clips to a movie. You can fade audio clips in and out for a more professional touch. Audio clips might serve as background music, sound effects, or narration.

Mix Audio in the Soundtrack

DRAG AUDIO CLIPS TO THE TIMELINE

① Click **Audio**.

The Audio pane opens.

● You can click here and select a collection from your iTunes library as well as other audio collections.

② Click and drag an audio clip from the Audio pane to the Timeline.

The song appears in the Timeline below any movie clips already in the movie.

EDIT AN AUDIO CLIP

● Click and drag an audio clip to reposition it in the Timeline.

● Click and drag the endpoints of an audio clip to mark where playback should begin and end for the clip.

Dragging inward from the edge of a clip shortens it; dragging an edge outward lengthens the clip.

FADE IN AN AUDIO CLIP

1. Click an audio clip in the Timeline to select it.

2. Click **View**.

3. Click **Show Clip Volume Levels**.

● A horizontal line appears on top of the audio clip, representing the volume of the clip at any point in time.

4. Click the **Volume line** to add a handle.

5. Drag the handle to the bottom of the Timeline to silence the clip.

6. Click the **Volume line** to add another handle directly to the right of the first handle.

7. Move the new handle toward the top of the Timeline to increase the volume.

On playback, the volume fades in.

 TIPS

Where can I find sound effects for my movie?

In the pop-up menu at the top of the Audio pane, you can find a popup menu item entitled **iMovie Sound Effects**. This section displays many sound effects that you can use in the background of your movie to give it realism. You can find animal noises, applause sounds, and other useful effects in the Audio pane.

How do I narrate over a movie?

You can connect a microphone to your Macintosh. If your Mac has a built-in microphone, you can use it instead. Next, select the microphone input in the Sound pane in the System Preferences. Finally, click **Record** at the bottom of the iMovie **Audio** pane to record your voice as the video plays. The Record button in the Audio pane is circular with a red dot at its center.

Add Professional-Looking Titles

Every professional movie begins by displaying its title as well as the names of directors, producers, and actors. You can add text titles to your movie for a professional look. Titles in iMovie can appear on a black background or over a movie clip. You can also change the font size, style, and color of titles to match your preferences.

ADD A TITLE

① Click **Titles**.

The Titles pane appears.

② Type the name of the movie in the Titles fields on the Titles pane.

③ Click **Over black** (☐ changes to ☑).

This option causes the title to appear on a black background; when deselected, iMovie superimposes the title over a movie clip.

④ Click an animation effect.

The preview window displays the animation.

⑤ Drag the effect to the Timeline.

The new title appears in the video track of the Timeline.

EDIT A TITLE IN THE TIMELINE

1 Click a title clip to select it.

2 Drag the **Size** slider () to the right.

3 Click **Preview**.

The text size in the thumbnail preview increases.

4 Click ⬍ and select a font.

This example selects Times New Roman.

The font in the Preview window changes to the font you selected.

5 Click **Update**.

iMovie updates the clip with the changes you made.

TIP

What does the QT margins option in the Titles pane do?

Computer displays and televisions screens differ in many significant ways. Computer displays can display the entire width and height of a movie. Televisions, on the other hand, have a tendency to cut off a small strip around the edges of the screen. Leave **QT margins** deselected if you want to view the movie on a television screen. This ensures that your title will not get cut off during viewing. If you only plan to watch the movie on a computer, select the **QT Margins** option (☐ changes to ☑). **QT Margins** give you the widest amount of screen space to display a title.

Movie transitions cause two clips to merge together visually in different interesting ways. You can add transitions between movie clips in the Timeline to simulate time passing or a change in location. You can change the speed and length of a transition. iMovie offers a selection of different types of transitions.

Add Visual Interest to Movies with Transitions

① Click **Trans**.

② Click a transition.

● A preview of the transition appears here.

③ In the Timeline, select two adjacent clips by holding down **Shift** and clicking each clip.

Depending on the type of transition, you can insert transitions at the beginning of a clip, at the end of a clip, or between two clips.

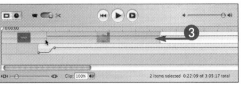

④ Click **Apply**.

● iMovie inserts the transition between the two selected clips.

EDIT A TRANSITION

① Click the transition in the Timeline.

② Click and drag ▣ to change the duration of the transition.

③ Click **Update**.

iMovie updates the transition to reflect its new settings.

TIP

How often should I use transitions, and which kinds should I use?

Although transitions give your movies a professional edge, overusing them can make movies look amateurish. Use transition effects sparingly for the best results. Use the Fade In and Fade Out transitions at the beginning and end of a movie. These transitions act like the curtain on a stage, opening and closing a performance. Dissolve transitions can give a movie a sentimental mood or even a sad feeling. Use the Cross Dissolve transition for a subtle, but effective way to show the passage of time. Absence of a transition between two clips is actually a type of transition too! Movie editors call this transition a *cut*. Cuts are abrupt and in wide use for a multitude of functions. They succeed at focusing attention quickly and directly from one topic to another.

Add Special Effects

You can add special effects to video clips in the iMovie HD Timeline. You can add grainy film effects or make it rain with the built-in iMovie HD effects. You can also apply multiple effects to the same clip for new combinations. If you decide that you do not like an effect, you can undo the effect immediately after applying it.

Add Special Effects

ADD A RAIN EFFECT

① In the Timeline, click a clip to select it.

② Click **Effects**.

The Effects pane opens.

③ Click **Rain** in the list of effects.

● The Preview area displays the clip with rain superimposed.

④ Drag ⊙ to adjust the look of the Rain effect.

⑤ Click **Apply**.

iMovie applies the rain effect to the clip.

ADD A FILM EFFECT

① In the Timeline, click a clip to select it.

② Click **Aged Film**.

● The Preview area displays the clip with a film effect superimposed.

③ Click **Apply**.

iMovie applies the Aged Film effect to the clip.

TIPS

Can I edit an effect after I apply it to a clip?

You can click Undo in the Edit menu to remove an effect immediately after you apply it. If you discover that it is too late to undo an action, click **Advanced**, and then click **Restore Clip**. This function strips away any effects that you applied to a clip and returns the clip to its unaffected state.

How many effects can I apply to a single clip?

You can apply an unlimited number of effects to any movie clip. You can even apply the same effect to a clip multiple times. Because editing is performed digitally, there is usually no degradation of quality as you add effects. If an effect causes the video to look degraded, however, multiple applications of the effect may have deleterious effects on its visual quality. For some applications, this may even be desirable. Experimentation goes a long way towards finding unique uses for effects.

Share the Movie

After you create a movie, the final step is to share it with others. You can share the movie over email or in a Web page. You can also transfer the movie back to a video camera. For more advanced needs, you can export a movie using one of the many exporters in QuickTime.

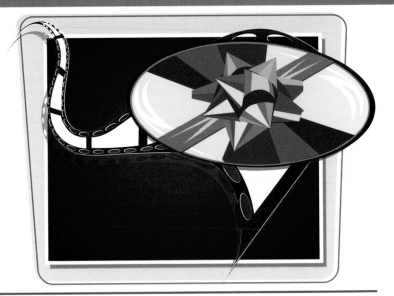

EXPORT A MOVIE FOR EMAIL

1. Click **File**.
2. Click **Share**.

   The Share sheet opens.

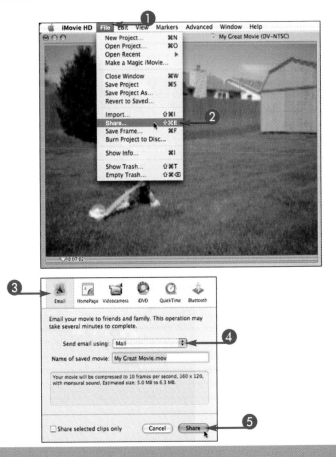

3. Click **Email**.

   The Email settings appear.
4. Click ⬛ and select **Mail**.
5. Click **Share**.

   iMovie exports the movie and attaches it to a new email message.

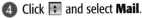

EXPORT A MOVIE FOR DISPLAY ON A WEB PAGE

① Click **File**.

② Click **Share**.

The Share sheet opens.

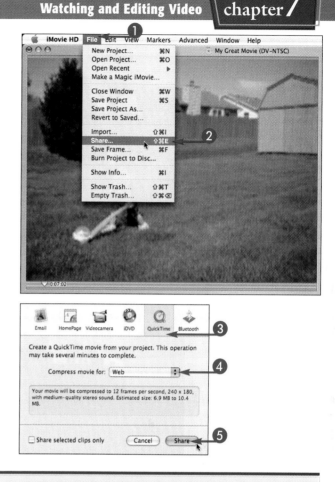

③ Click **QuickTime**.

The QuickTime settings appear.

④ Click 🔧 and select **Web**.

⑤ Click **Share**.

iMovie exports a movie file that is appropriate for a Web page and asks where you want to save it.

What does Expert Settings in the QuickTime Share settings do?

Expert Settings provides you with a way to share a movie file in any of the formats that QuickTime permits. It works identically to the QuickTime Player Export settings. You can choose a format for the export operation. For video, you might select **Movie to MPEG-4** or **Movie to QuickTime Movie**.

Then, you can adjust specific settings like quality and size, depending on which format you choose. To adjust format-specific settings, click **Options**.

Can I transfer a movie back to a video camera?

Yes. iMovie enables you to share a movie with a camera. Transferring a movie to a camera is useful, because you can use the camera to play the movie on a television or to transfer it to a videocassette. To transfer a movie from your Mac to a video camera, click **File**, then click **Share**. In the Share sheet, click **Videocamera** in the Toolbar across the top of the sheet. Finally, click the **Share** button to transfer the video to a video camera.

Harnessing the Power of the Internet

The Internet offers an abundance of information, but it is also complex. Mac OS X Tiger eases your introduction to this world by including a set of useful Internet tools that help you surf the Web, send and receive email, and read RSS news feeds.

Safari is the OS X Web browser made by Apple. You can load a Web page in Safari and scroll the page up and down with keystrokes as you read it. The SnapBack option gives you quick access to a previous page that you can set.

LOAD A WEB PAGE

1 In the Dock, click **Safari**.

The Safari Web browser launches.

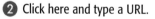

2 Click here and type a URL.

3 Press Return .

Safari loads and displays the Web page at that address.

NAVIGATE A WEB PAGE

Press  to scroll down the page a short distance.

Press ⬆ to scroll back up the same distance.

Press **Spacebar** to scroll down the length of the current window's content area.

Press **Shift** + **Spacebar** to scroll up one page length.

④ Click a link.

Safari loads the page associated with the link.

REVISIT A PAGE WITH SNAPBACK

⑤ Click **SnapBack** (🔄).

Safari returns to the first Web page.

Note: Clicking 🔄 displays the page at the URL you most recently typed in the Address bar, including bookmarks, bypassing all intermediate sites that you accessed by clicking links.

TIPS

How do I specify a SnapBack page?

If you want to reset the SnapBack to another page, click **History**, and then click **Mark Page for SnapBack**.

How can I open a link in a new window?

You can open a link in a new window by pressing and holding ⌘ while you click the link. If you have Tabs enabled, the link opens in a new tab of the same window instead. ⌘ + **Option**-clicking a link opens it in a new window with Tabs enabled.

Block Pop-up Windows

Advertisers that clutter your Desktop with pop-up windows can be an annoying part of Web surfing. Pop-up windows can cause problems, because they force you to interact with a window other than the one you had intended to use. Some advertisers are particularly aggressive with pop-ups, causing your browser to become unresponsive. You can block pop-up windows in Safari and eliminate the problems they cause.

Block Pop-Up Windows

① In Safari, click **Safari**.

② Click **Block Pop-Up Windows**.

Safari prevents most pop-up windows from opening.

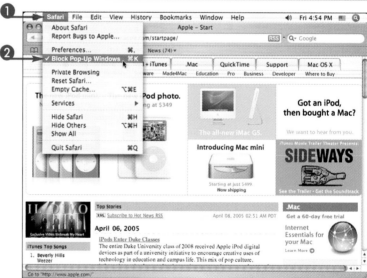

DISABLE POP-UP WINDOWS IN THE PREFERENCES

① Press ⌘+@@.

The Preferences window opens.

② Click **Security**.

③ Click **Block pop-up windows** (☐ changes to ☑).

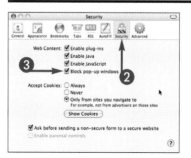

Google.com is, perhaps, the single most popular search engine on the Internet — and for good reason. Google has a simple, but effective, interface and its search results are excellent. In Safari, you can search the Internet with its built-in Google features. To save time, you can save searches and return to them later.

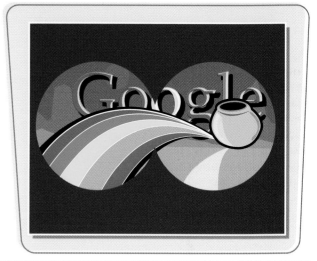

Search Google

FIND A WEB SITE

1. In Safari, click in the Google field and type a phrase.

2. Press **Return**.

   Safari queries Google and displays the search results.

RETURN TO A PREVIOUS SEARCH

1. Click 🔍.

   A pop-up menu opens, displaying previous Google searches.

2. Click a previous search to repeat the search.

   Google displays the search results in the Safari window.

Surf with Tabs

As you open more windows to load Web pages in Safari, the interface can quickly become cluttered. Safari solves this problem with Tabs. Each window can contain any number of Tabs. Each Tab can display a different Web page. You can load your Web pages into Tabs, which reduces screen clutter and helps you find information more quickly.

Surf with Tabs

ACTIVATE TABBED BROWSING

① Click **Safari**.

② Click **Preferences**.

The Preferences window opens.

③ Click **Tabs**.

④ Click **Enable Tabbed Browsing**
(☐ changes to ☑).

Activating tabbed browsing changes some Safari keyboard shortcuts, which are listed at the bottom of the Preferences window.

⑤ Click **Always show tab bar** option
(☐ changes to ☑).

⑥ Click Close.

The Preferences window closes.

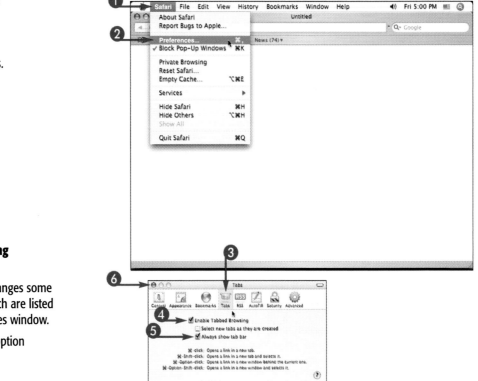

SAVE A WEB PAGE AS A PDF

1. Load a Web page in Safari.

2. Click **File**.

3. Click **Print**.

   The Print dialog box appears.

4. Click **PDF**.

5. Click **Save As PDF**.

   The Save As dialog box appears.

6. Type a name for the PDF file.

7. Click ▲ and select a folder in which to save the Web page.

8. Click **Save**.

   Safari creates a PDF file of the page.

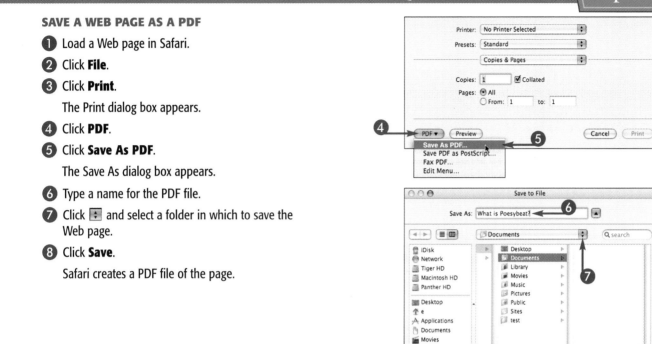

TIPS

What is the difference between saving a Web page as an archive and saving one as a PDF file?

When you save a Web page as an archive, Safari saves the Web page and its images into an archive file and maintains clickable links in the process. Saving as a PDF wraps the whole page in a PDF graphics file. This is useful for viewing on other platforms like Microsoft Windows.

In what format should I save a Web page if I do not care about images?

You can save a Web page in **Page Source** format. The Page Source format maintains the formatting of the original Web page, but it only saves text from the page. For example, if the Web page is composed of HTML, when you save as Page Source, the resulting file will contain HTML text and nothing else. This is sufficient for viewing its data later, but will not include any images from the original Web page.

Send an Email Message

Mail is the email application in Mac OS X Tiger. You can send email with Mail to one or multiple recipients. For multiple recipients, you can hide email addresses from other recipients to maintain privacy.

Send an Email Message

LAUNCH MAIL

① In the Dock, click **Mail**.

The Mail application launches.

② If you do not see a Viewer window, click **File**.

③ Click **New Viewer Window**.

A new Viewer window opens.

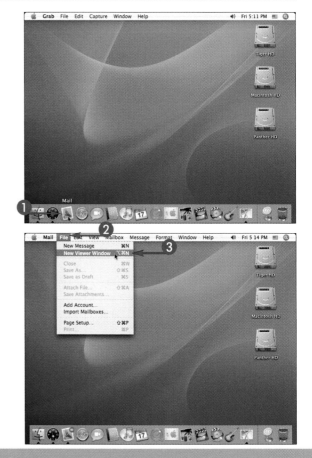

CREATE A NEW EMAIL MESSAGE

① Click **File**.

② Click **New Message**.

Mail opens a new message window.

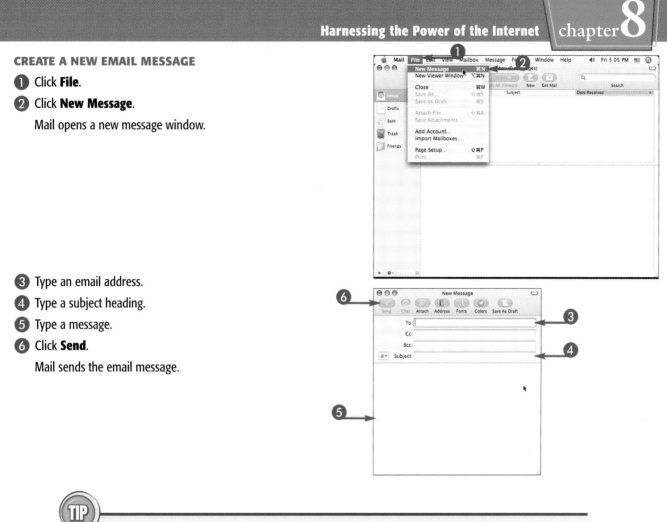

③ Type an email address.

④ Type a subject heading.

⑤ Type a message.

⑥ Click **Send**.

Mail sends the email message.

TIP

Can I send an email to more than one person?

Yes. You can type multiple email addresses in the **To**, **CC**, and **BCC** fields separated by commas. CC and BCC stand for "carbon copy" and "blind carbon copy," respectively. You can activate BCC by clicking **View**, then clicking **BCC Header**. When you CC an email address, Mail sends a copy of the email to that address and displays that CC information in the email. When you type an address in the BCC field, Mail sends a copy of the email to that address, but it does not display the BCC information in the email. Thus the recipients of this email do not know that the addresses in the BCC field also received a copy of the message.

Read Email Messages

You can read and organize your email messages in Mail. Mail has functions to help you organize email into folders. You can also flag especially important emails to help you find them easily later. As emails fill your Inbox, you can follow within the same thread by looking for emails that are similarly colored.

Read Email Messages

VIEW AN EMAIL

① In Mail, click **Inbox**.

Mail displays all email messages in the Inbox.

② Click a message.

● Mail displays the email message in the bottom pane.

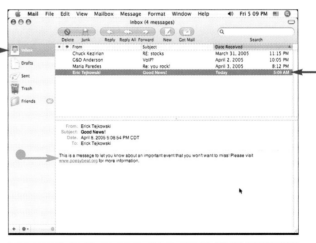

ORGANIZE EMAIL

① Click the **New Mailbox** (+) button.

The New Mailbox dialog box appears.

② Click ⊟ and select **On My Mac**.

③ Type a name for the mailbox.

④ Click **OK**.

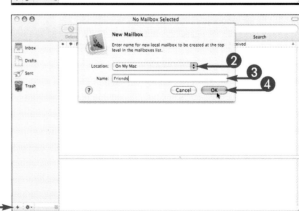

A new mailbox folder appears in the Mailboxes drawer.

⑤ Click **Inbox**.

⑥ Click and drag an email message from the Inbox to the newly created mailbox folder.

● Click the new mailbox folder to view its contents.

Why are some email messages marked with different colors when I click them?

Mail denotes messages within the same thread by marking them with the same color. This helps you locate related messages quickly and easily. For example, Mail marks a message brown if it considers it SPAM.

How do I mark important messages?

You can mark a message as "flagged" by selecting it in the viewer window and pressing ⌘ + Shift + L. Mail marks flagged messages with a flag icon. The icon can help you quickly locate important messages visually. You can also sort all messages based on if they are flagged or not, so you can view all flagged messages together.

Work with Email Attachments

Mail gives you a few different options for handling file attachments. When you need to send a file to someone, you can attach it to a message and email it. When someone sends you an attachment, you can either save it to your hard drive or open it immediately.

ATTACH A FILE TO AN EMAIL MESSAGE

① In Mail, create a new message by pressing ⌘ + N.

A new message window appears.

② Click **Attach**.

An Open File sheet appears.

③ Click a file that you want to attach to the message.

④ Click **Choose File**.

The file attachment appears in the message.

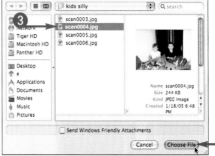

SAVE AN ATTACHMENT

① Open a message that contains an attachment.

② Click **Save**.

③ Click **Save All**.

The Save dialog box appears.

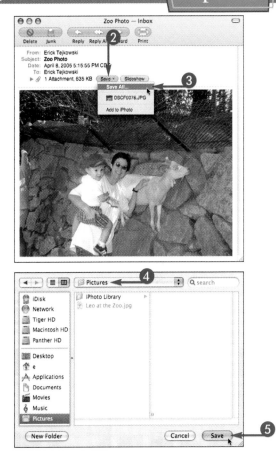

④ Select the folder where you want to save the attached file.

⑤ Click **Save**.

Mail saves the attached file in the chosen folder.

TIPS

What does the Slideshow button do?

When an email message contains image attachments, you can view them within Mail as a slideshow. Click the **Slideshow** button to view the image attachments in that email as a full-screen slideshow. You can manually thumb through images, pause the slideshow to look at a particular photo, or let it run automatically, changing photos intermittently.

Can I use the drag-and-drop feature with attachments?

You can drag and drop files into an email message. If the attachment is an image, like a JPEG or PDF file, the image appears in the body of the email. Some media files like QuickTime movies and audio files cause a media player to appear in the email. Otherwise, a file icon appears in the message body.

Delete an Email Message

To save hard drive space and for security reasons, you may not want to keep every email message that you receive. Deleting old email messages — especially from your Inbox — enables you to more quickly find messages you want because it leaves you with less clutter. You can delete email messages in Mail in much the same way that you delete files in the Finder.

Delete an Email Message

MOVE A FILE TO THE TRASH WITH THE KEYBOARD

① In Mail, click a message to select it.

② Press Delete.

● Mail moves the message to the Trash folder.

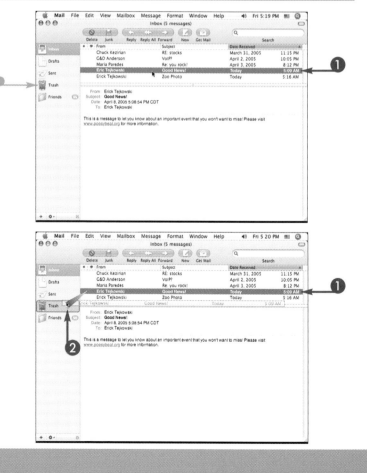

DRAG AN EMAIL TO THE TRASH

① Click an email message to select it.

② Drag the email to the Trash folder.

Mail moves the email from the Inbox to the Trash folder.

RETRIEVE AN EMAIL FROM THE TRASH

1 Click **Trash**.

Mail displays the Trash folder contents.

2 Click and drag an email from the Trash to another folder in the Viewer window.

Mail moves the email from the Trash folder to the Inbox.

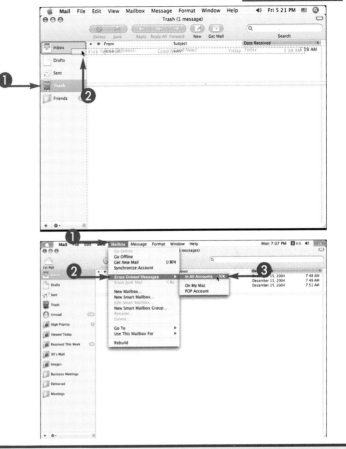

EMPTY THE MAIL TRASH

1 Click **Mailbox**.

2 Click **Erase Deleted Messages**.

3 Click **In All Accounts**.

Mail permanently removes all messages from the Trash folder.

Are there any other ways that I can delete a message?

You can also click and drag email messages to the Trash icon in the Dock. When you do, the message appears in the Trash folder in Mail. If you mistakenly delete a message, you can undo the action by pressing ⌘+Z. The deleted email message reappears in the mailbox that it was in originally.

When I delete an email message, Mail automatically displays the next message in the Inbox. How can I prevent this behavior?

For security reasons, you may not want to automatically view the next message in the mailbox when you delete a message. To prevent Mail from displaying the next email, press and hold Option while clicking the **Delete** button in the toolbar. Mail deletes the message and does not display another email in the main window. You can also resize the viewing pane and only open messages in their own window by double-clicking them. This permits you to select a message for deletion without actually viewing the message first.

Eliminate Spam from Your Inbox

Spam is unsolicited and unwanted email that appears in your Inbox. Mail has sophisticated technology that helps you spot and remove spam, which Apple calls Junk Mail. You can also train it to recognize spam that it does not know already. To make it easy to spot email that is marked as spam, you can colorize individual messages with the color of your choice.

Eliminate Spam from Your Inbox

DESIGNATE EMAIL AS JUNK

1. In Mail, click **Inbox**.

   Mail displays the messages in your Inbox.

2. Click an email message that you consider to be spam.

3. Click **Junk**.

   Mail marks the message as Junk.

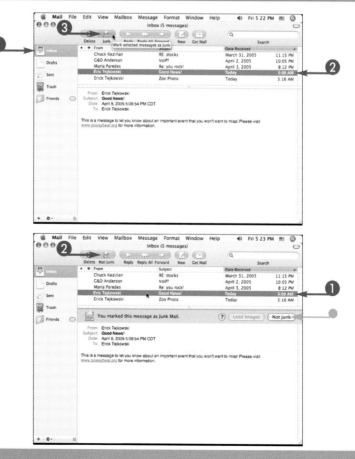

REMOVE THE JUNK MARKER FROM AN EMAIL

1. Select an email message marked as Junk that you consider not to be spam.

2. Click **Not Junk**.

- You can also click **Not Junk** in the message preview.

   Mail removes the coloring and markers from the message that indicate that it is junk mail.

FILTER JUNK MAIL

① Click **Mail**.

② Click **Preferences**.

The Preferences window opens.

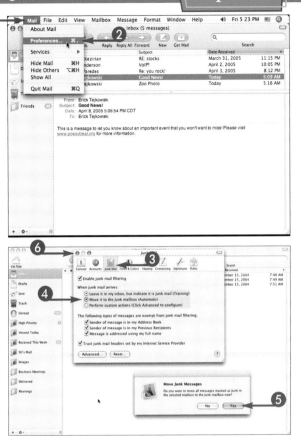

③ Click **Junk Mail**.

④ Click **Move it to the Junk mailbox (Automatic)** option (○ changes to ◉).

Mail asks you if you want to move all messages marked as Junk to the Junk Mailbox.

⑤ Click **Yes**.

⑥ Click 📧.

Mail moves all junk mail to the Junk Mailbox.

TIPS

Mail is improperly marking too many of my legitimate email messages as junk. What should I do?

In the Junk Mail pane of the Preferences window, select the **When Junk Mail arrives** to **Leave it in my Inbox, but indicate it is Junk Mail (Training)** option (○ changes to ◉). While in Training mode, Mail learns what you consider junk mail.

I do not like the brown color that Mail uses to mark junk mail. Can I change the color?

You can change the color that Mail uses to mark junk mail in the Preferences window. In the Junk Mail pane, click **Advanced** to open the sheet where the color setting resides. In the **Perform the following actions** section, click **Other** in the **Color** popup menu to select a color of your choice from the color picker.

CHAPTER

Connecting to Other Machines on a Network

You can connect to computers on a network to perform a variety of tasks. For example, the Finder lets you share files with Mac and Windows computers, and Tiger also has a built-in Web server, a firewall, and the ability to share printers. With iChat, you can chat with friends and exchange files, and iTunes lets you share your music across a network.

If you use a laptop computer, you may want to switch between your work or school network and your home network. You can define different locations in your Network settings, so that you can switch networks with one mouse click. As you switch between locations, you can use different types of network connections for each location. The Network pane can even assist you in the setup process.

Edit Network Settings

CREATE A LOCATION

① In the Dock, click **System Preferences**.

The System Preferences window opens.

② Click **Network**.

The Network pane opens.

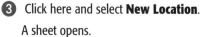

③ Click here and select **New Location**.

A sheet opens.

④ Type a name for the location.

⑤ Click **OK**.

You can now set up the network for this location, which now appears in the Network window.

CHANGE LOCATIONS

① Click 🍎.

② Click **Location**.

③ Click a location in the menu.

The network changes to use the new Location settings.

TIPS

What kind of network connection can I use in each location?

At work, you might use an Ethernet connection; at home, an AirPort connection; and while on the road, a modem. You can use any type of connection with any location, including IP over FireWire, which lets you create an IP network using only a FireWire cable between two Macs.

I do not feel comfortable setting up my own network. Where can I find help?

Click **Assist me** in the Network pane of the System Preferences window. This Network Setup Assistant guides you through the steps of setting up a network connection. It asks you to provide some information about your network configuration and gives you detailed instructions and descriptions for each step.

Share Files with Macs

You can share files with any Mac on your network. Sharing files over a network is often much quicker than burning a CD and transferring the data manually. To access shared files more quickly, you can create a shortcut to your favorite locations on the network.

Share Files with Macs

ACTIVATE FILE SHARING

1. In the Dock, click **System Preferences**.

   The System Preferences window opens.

2. Click **Sharing**.

   The Sharing Pane opens.

3. Click **Services**.

4. Click **Personal File Sharing** (☑ changes to ☐).

   File Sharing activates.

5. Click **Close**.

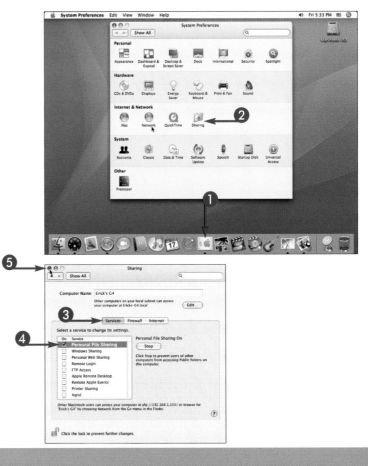

SHARE FILES

1 In the Finder, press ⌘+N.

A new Finder window opens.

2 Click **Network**.

The Network Browser opens, displaying the servers on the local network.

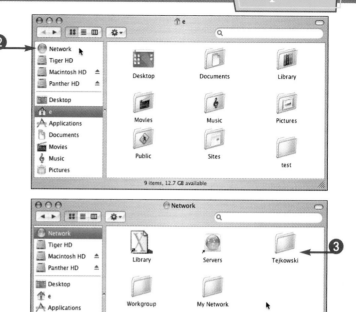

3 Double-click a server icon to log in and share files with it.

Why can I not view the items in the Drop Box of another computer?

The Drop Box is a folder into which other users can drop files. The Drop Box, however, does not normally permit you to view its contents unless you log in to that computer with the correct username and password for the Drop Box, or if the owner changes permissions. Guest access prevents you from viewing the contents of any Drop Box.

There are many steps involved in mounting a shared network folder. What would save me time?

Once you locate a folder that you want to share, you can create an alias to it by dragging it to your Desktop while pressing and holding ⌘+Option. The next time you want to put something in that Drop Box, it is instantly accessible.

Share Files with Windows Users

Macintosh is not the only operating system found on networks. Microsoft Windows also inhabits many networks alongside Macs. You can share many common types of files with Windows just as easily as you can share files with a Mac. Some files, like Macintosh applications, are not compatible with Windows computers.

Share Files with Windows Users

BROWSE FOR WINDOWS MACHINES

① In the Finder, click **File**.

② Click **New Finder Window**.

A new window opens.

③ Click **Network**.

The Finder displays file servers and computers that are sharing on the network.

④ Double-click a network area or workgroup to view its servers.

A solitary computer appears in this network area.

⑤ Double-click the server to connect to it.

An SMB Mount dialog box appears.

⑥ Click ⬦ and select a shared folder.

⑦ Click **OK**.

The Finder mounts the share just like any other drive on your system.

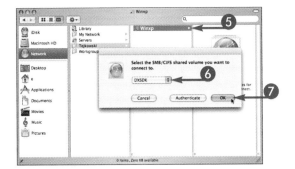

CONNECT DIRECTLY TO A WINDOWS COMPUTER

① In the Finder, click **Go**.

② Click **Connect to Server**.

The Connect to Server window opens.

③ Type the address of a shared Windows computer.

The format of the address is smb://WORKGROUP;
USERNAME:PASSWORD@ADDRESS, where you
replace WORKGROUP, USERNAME, PASSWORD, and
ADDRESS with your own information.

④ Click **Connect**.

A connection dialog box appears.

⑤ Click ▣ and select the shared folder that you want
to use.

⑥ Click **OK**.

The shared folder appears in the Finder as a hard
drive icon.

TIP

Are there any files I should be cautious of sharing with Windows users?

The only files you should take care in sharing
with Windows users are those that contain
resource forks. Resource forks are a leftover
byproduct of the Mac OS before OS X. While
they work fine in OS X, they are, generally
speaking, incompatible with Windows.
Most files that you share with Windows
users will not have resource forks. In
case you are not sure if a file has a
resource fork, you can always archive a file
in the Finder before transferring it to a
Windows computer.

There are millions of Web servers in existence. You can join them on the Internet by running the Apache Web server that is built into Mac OS X Tiger. All users can serve their own Web pages on the same machine.

Run a Web Server

LAUNCH THE WEB SERVER

① In the Dock, click **System Preferences**.

The System Preferences window opens.

② Click **Sharing**.

The Sharing dialog box appears.

③ Click **Personal Web Sharing** (☐ changes to ☑).

The Web server is now active.

④ Click one of the two links.

A Web browser opens the page at the URL that you click.

● The URL you clicked appears in the browser's Address field.

Where do I place files so that they may be viewed with a Web browser?

You can place files in one of two locations. The current user has a Web page that is located in the Sites folder of the Home folder. The computer also has a Web page allocated to it. You can find it in /Library/WebServer/ Documents. Place Web pages in either of these folders to view them through the Web server.

What is Apache?

Apache is the name of popular Web server software. It is also the software that drives the Personal Web Sharing feature in Mac OS X. Apache is considered stable and robust software and is used in a majority of Web servers on the World Wide Web. You can find a wealth of information about the Apache Web server at http://httpd. apache.org.

Protect Your Network with a Firewall

When you connect to the Internet, you should take care to protect your computer from outside intruders. A firewall is a hardware or software device that prevents outsiders from gaining access to your network or computer. Mac OS X Tiger has a built-in firewall that you can use to protect your computer. Sometimes you need to bypass the firewall. You can customize your firewall settings to share music over a network.

Protect Your Network with a Firewall

ACTIVATE THE FIREWALL

1 In the Dock, click **System Preferences**.

The System Preferences window opens.

2 Click **Sharing**.

The Sharing dialog box appears.

3 Click the **Firewall** tab.

The Firewall tab opens.

4 Click **Start**.

Mac OS X starts the firewall.

ENABLE ITUNES MUSIC SHARING

⑤ Click **iTunes Music Sharing** (☐ changes to ☑).

The firewall continues operating, but permits iTunes traffic to pass through it.

BLOCK ACCESS TO FIREWALL SETTINGS

① In the Firewall pane of the Sharing window, click **Click the lock to make changes** (🔒 changes to 🔓).

🔒 indicates that the firewall is locked. When you unlock it, a Mac OS X asks you for an administrator password.

TIPS

What does a firewall do?

A firewall blocks incoming traffic from entering your network. It does not, however, block outgoing traffic, which means you can continue to browse the Web or read email without problems. To permit incoming traffic to pass, you can open a channel, called a *port,* in your firewall. You generally do not need to open a port unless you are running a server.

I have a hardware router with a built-in firewall. Do I need to use the firewall in both the router and the System Preferences?

If you have a hardware router, you should discontinue use of the built-in firewall in OS X. Two firewalls are not better than one, because the combination can interfere with each other and block traffic that you want to pass.

QuickTime has the ability to stream audio, video, and text data across the Internet to your QuickTime Player or Web browser. To ensure the best listening and viewing experience, you can adjust speed settings in the QuickTime pane of the System Preferences window, in QuickTime Player, and in the QuickTime Plug-in. Servers can customize the files you download, based on your connection speed.

Set QuickTime Network Connection Speed

SET THE SPEED IN THE SYSTEM PREFERENCES

① In the Dock, click **System Preferences**.

The System Preferences window opens.

② Click **QuickTime**.

The QuickTime pane opens.

③ Click **Streaming**.

④ Click ▣ and choose a Streaming Speed.

⑤ Click ◉.

The System Preferences window closes.

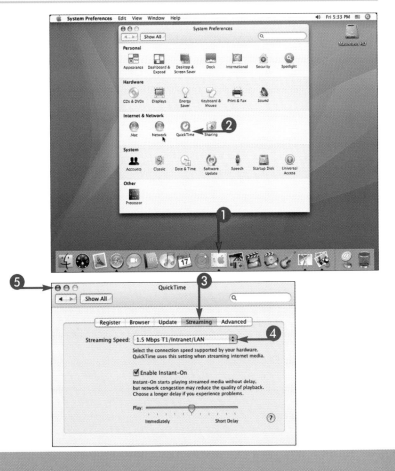

ACCESS QUICKTIME SETTINGS IN SAFARI

① In the Dock, click **Safari** to launch it.

② Load a Web page that contains a QuickTime movie.

The QuickTime plug-in in Safari plays the movie at the dimensions and file size appropriate for your Internet connection.

Note: Visit www.apple.com/trailers for a list of new movie trailers.

③ Click **Connection Speed** in the player's pop-up menu.

The QuickTime pane of the System Preferences opens for you to set the connection speed.

ACCESS QUICKTIME SETTINGS IN QUICKTIME PLAYER

① In the Dock, click **QuickTime Player**.

QuickTime Player launches.

② Click **QuickTime Player**.

③ Click **QuickTime Preferences**.

The QuickTime pane of the System Preferences opens where you can set the connection speed.

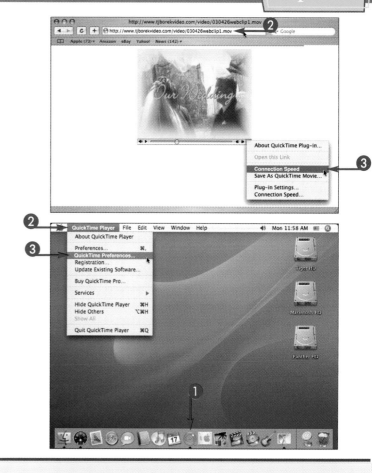

TIPS

What happens if I set a connection speed that is too high?

If you set a connection speed that is too high, you may have to wait longer for the larger movie file to download to your computer. However, the quality of the final result will be high.

What does the QuickTime Instant-On setting do?

QuickTime can begin playing streaming media as soon as it arrives at your computer. If the network is slow or congested, this can cause playback problems that result in stuttering or skipping audio. The Instant-On setting gives you the chance to adjust how long QuickTime waits before it begins playback. Longer delays help reduce problems of stuttering audio.

You can share a printer with many different computers on a network. To begin sharing a printer, you must activate printer sharing in the System Preferences. When sharing a printer, print jobs are queued up in the order in which the printer receives them.

Share a Printer

START PRINTER SHARING

① In the Dock, click **System Preferences**.

The System Preferences window opens.

② Click **Sharing**.

The Sharing window appears.

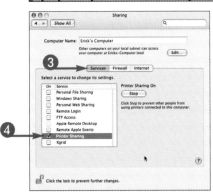

③ Click the **Services** tab.

④ Click **Printer Sharing** (changes to).

Note: Alternatively, you can click Printer Sharing and then click the Start button to enable printer sharing.

Mac OS X starts Printer Sharing.

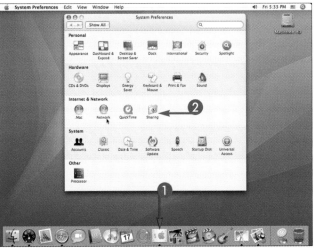

PRINT TO A SHARED PRINTER

① Open a document in TextEdit.

② Click **File**.

③ Click **Print**.

The Print dialog box opens.

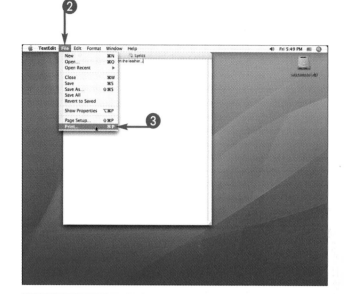

④ Click ⬧ and select **Shared Printers**.

If someone is using Panther or Jaguar to print to a shared printer, the option reads "Rendezvous Printers" instead of "Shared Printers."

⑤ Click ⬧ and select a shared printer.

⑥ Click **Print**.

The document prints on the shared printer.

Can more than one computer print to a shared printer?

Multiple computers can print to the same printer. The Print Center utility queues the print jobs in the order in which it receives them. As it receives print jobs, it begins printing the documents. When one print job is complete, Print Center continues printing any additional jobs left in the queue until all print jobs are finished.

What kinds of printers can I share on a network?

You can print to a wide array of shared printers on a network. Most Macintosh printers connect to computers via USB. Windows printers, however, often use parallel ports to connect to a computer. Some printers connect directly to the network using an Ethernet cable. You can print from OS X to shared printers that use USB, parallel, FireWire, and Ethernet connections.

Add an iChat Buddy

iChat is an OS X application that lets you communicate with people all over the world. iChat keeps track of your friends and family in a Buddy List. You can add an iChat Buddy for any person either manually or from an entry in your address book. To use iChat outside of your local network, you must register with an AIM or .Mac account. Bonjour chatting does not require any account registration, but limits chats to within your local home or office network.

Add an iChat Buddy

LAUNCH ICHAT

1 In the Dock, click **iChat**.

The iChat window appears.

If the Buddy List does not appear, press ⌘+1 to display the list.

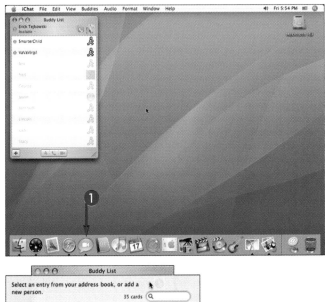

ADD A NEW BUDDY FROM THE ADDRESS BOOK

1 Click ➕.

iChat displays a list of contacts from your Address Book.

2 Click a person who has an entry in the Instant Messaging column.

3 Click **Select Buddy**.

iChat adds the person to the Buddy List.

ADD A NEW BUDDY MANUALLY

① Click (⊞).

iChat displays a list of contacts from your Address Book.

② Click **New Person**.

iChat opens a sheet where you can add a new buddy.

③ Click ⬍ and select an account type.

If the buddy uses the .Mac network, click **.Mac;** if the buddy uses an AOL Instant Messenger screen name, click **AIM**.

④ Type the account name.

If you want, you can also type the name and email address of the buddy.

⑤ Click **Add**.

iChat adds the buddy to the Buddy List.

Where can I register for an AIM account?

To register an AIM screen name, visit the AOL Instant Messenger Web site at www.aim.com. An AIM account is sometimes preferable to a .Mac account, because registration is free and because you can use the same account on a Microsoft Windows machine.

Where can I register for a .Mac account?

To register a .Mac screen name, visit the .Mac Web site at **www.mac.com**. Some users prefer a .Mac iChat username instead of an AIM account, because it comes bundled with the purchase of a .Mac account.

Send Instant Messages with iChat

You can send messages to friends and family with iChat. Each message can contain formatted text, images, and emoticons. Emoticons are small icons that are supposed to denote an emotion. Common emoticons are smiley and frowny faces. When you are finished chatting, you can save the chat session to a file for later viewing.

Send Instant Messages with iChat

SEND A SIMPLE MESSAGE

① In the Dock, click **iChat** .

The iChat Buddy window appears.

② In your Buddy List, double-click a name.

● A new chat window opens.

③ Type a message.

④ Press **Return** .

● iChat sends the message to the recipient and waits for confirmation.

● Your buddy replies and the chat session begins.

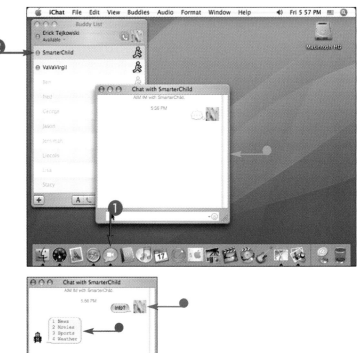

FORMAT A MESSAGE

1 In a chat window, type a message, but do not press Return.

2 Select a portion of the message.

3 Click **Format**.

4 Click **Bold**.

The selected text that you typed appears bold.

5 Press Return.

The typed message is sent to your buddy.

INSERT A SMILEY FACE

1 In a chat window, click the smiley face (⊡) at the right of the text input area.

2 Choose an emoticon from the pop-up menu that appears.

● An icon appears in the chat window with the emoticon that you chose.

TIPS

Can I save chats for later viewing?

You can save chats by pressing ⌘+S. This saves the entire conversation you had in a .chat file. Later, you can double-click this file to view its contents with iChat. You can also copy text from a chat window and paste it into a document in another application, like TextEdit, to save it there.

SHORT CUT

click

S   cmd

Can I use other kinds of faces in my chats? What are the keystrokes for each face?

iChat provides you with 16 different faces in the field where you type the message. When you click the smiley face, a pop-up menu shows you the faces and keystrokes required to produce those faces.

In addition to exchanging text messages, you can send files with iChat. You can insert pictures or any other file directly into a chat window to send it. Alternatively, you can bypass the chat window altogether, and drag a file directly from your desktop to your buddy's name in the Buddy list.

Send a File with iChat

SEND A FILE IN THE CHAT WINDOW

1 Initiate a chat with a buddy.

Note: To initiate a chat, see the section "Send Instant Messages with iChat."

2 Click and drag a file from the Finder into the message field.

The file's icon appears in the message field.

3 Press .

iChat tells the buddy that a file is forthcoming, and you must wait until the buddy accepts the file before it begins to transfer.

SEND A FILE WITH THE BUDDY LIST

① Click **Window**.

② Click **Buddy List**.

The Buddy List opens.

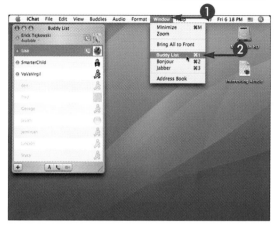

③ Click and drag a file from the Finder onto the name of a buddy in the Buddy List.

iChat initiates a file transfer as soon as the buddy accepts the file.

When I click and drag an image file like a JPEG into the message field, it appears as a miniature version of the image, but no file transfer occurs. What's wrong?

When you click and drag an image file into iChat, the image appears in the chat session. Your buddy can still download the file by clicking and dragging it from his chat window to his Desktop.

Are there any other ways to send files with iChat?

You can `Control`-click a name in the Buddy List to open a pop-up menu. Click the **Send a File** option. With this option, select a file to send through the standard Open dialog box. Then, click the **Open** button. iChat initiates a transfer of the selected file.

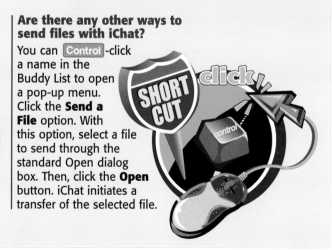

CHAPTER

10

Utilities

Mac OS X Tiger has a large collection of important utilities. You can troubleshoot problems, take screen shots, monitor the system, and automate your work with the utilities that Tiger provides.

Monitor CPU Usage

When your computer's responsiveness decreases substantially, the problem can often be attributed to an application that has gone awry. An errant application can overrun the CPU and prevent other applications from using it. You can monitor how hard your Mac is working with Activity Monitor to reveal any applications that might be overloading the CPU.

LAUNCH ACTIVITY MONITOR

① In the Finder, click **Go**.

② Click **Utilities**.

The Utilities window opens.

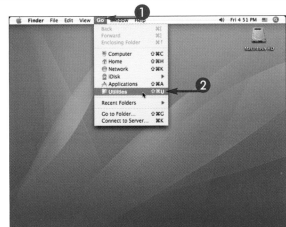

③ Double-click **Activity Monitor** to launch it.

MONITOR CPU ACTIVITY

① In the Activity Monitor window, click here and select **My Processes**.

② Click the **CPU** tab.

③ Click the **% CPU** tab.

Activity Monitor sorts the list of running processes according to CPU activity.

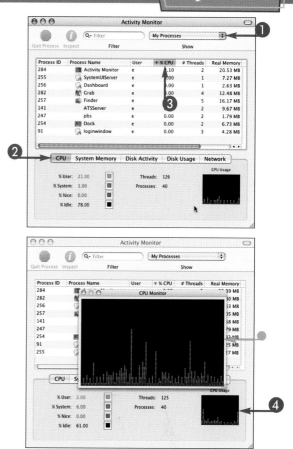

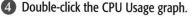

④ Double-click the CPU Usage graph.

● A new window opens that displays the CPU Monitor graph updating in real time.

Does a high % CPU guarantee that an application is frozen?

While a high % CPU value is a symptom of a frozen application, it is not necessarily a guaranteed indicator. Some applications temporarily spike in CPU activity depending on the amount of work each is doing. To make sure that an application is really frozen, you can Option -click its icon in the Dock to open its popup menu. Applications that are frozen display "Application not Responding" in their Dock popup menus.

What does the CPU do?

CPU is short for Central Processing Unit. It is the microprocessor chip in your computer that does all of the "thinking." You can think of it as the brain of your computer. At its lowest level, a CPU performs millions of mathematical computations — each second. The results of these computations are what make a computer perform tasks like loading a web page, showing a screensaver, or playing a game.

Stop Errant Applications

Humans write computer software, and as a result, software can sometimes not perform up to expectations. When an application freezes your computer and prevents you from working with your computer optimally, you can locate the problematic software and force it to stop running. This permits you to continue working without rebooting the computer. It also helps you prevent loss of data, since all other applications continue running.

Stop Errant Applications

QUIT A PROCESS

① Locate a problematic application in **Activity Monitor** and click it.

Note: To launch Activity Monitor, see the section "Monitor CPU Usage."

Those processes with the highest % CPU values require the most amount of work from your CPU, so a value that seems excessive is a likely suspect.

② Click **Quit Process**.

Activity Monitor asks you to confirm that you really want to quit the process.

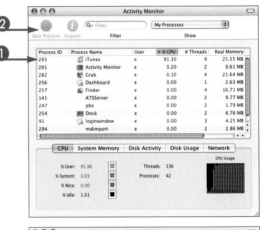

③ Click **Quit**.

Activity Monitor forces the troublesome process to quit.

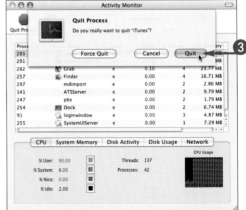

SAVE A LIST OF PROCESSES

1 Click **File**.

2 Click **Save**.

The Save sheet opens.

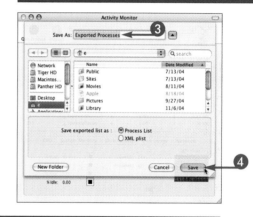

3 Type a name for the file.

4 Click **Save**.

Activity Monitor exports a list of the current processes that you can view at a later date.

TIP

Is it safe to quit any application?

Some processes have cryptic names that do not describe the application to which they belong. If you are not absolutely positive that a process is safe to quit, you should avoid doing so. Although you probably will not encounter any problems should you force-quit an application, you do risk losing data in any applications that are running. To ensure that this does not happen, quit all running applications first and then quit the offending process. If it makes your machine unstable, you might need to log out or reboot the machine, but this is not usually necessary.

Watch Network Activity

Sometimes network activity can overpower your computer and make it perform sluggishly. You can watch the activity on your network with Activity Monitor to ascertain if the network is the cause of sluggishness. You can display network activity in the Activity Monitor interface or in its Dock icon. You can also customize the manner in which activity Monitor displays the network data.

Watch Network Activity

VIEW THE NETWORK ACTIVITY GRAPH

① In Activity Monitor, click the **Network** tab.

Note: *To launch Activity Monitor, see the section "Monitor CPU Usage."*

Activity Monitor displays a graph of the network activity with two colored lines that represent incoming and outgoing data.

CUSTOMIZE COLOR SETTINGS

② Click the **Data received/sec** color button.

A standard color palette appears.

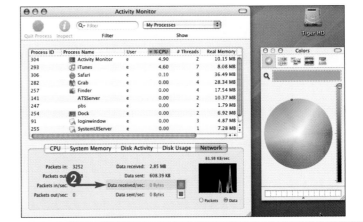

③ Select a new color.

● The graph changes to the color your selected.

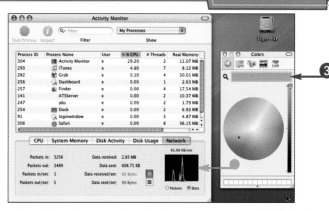

DISPLAY NETWORK ACTIVITY IN THE DOCK

① Click the **Activity Monitor** icon in the Dock and continue holding the mouse button.

A contextual menu opens.

② Click **Dock Icon**.

③ Click **Show Network Usage**.

The Network Monitor graph appears in the Dock icon.

TIPS

I am not surfing the Internet, but my network activity is still high. Why?

Web browsers are not the only applications that can cause network activity to spike. Email, iChat, Terminal, network printing and items in the Sharing pane of the System Preferences are all capable of causing network traffic to increase. Before you assume that someone is hacking into your computer, make sure that no other application might be causing the spike.

Why does my network connection seem to download so much faster than it uploads?

Many ISPs (Internet service providers) provide faster download speeds than upload speeds, presumably to combat piracy of music, video, and software files, which tend to be large. Nothing is wrong with your Macintosh. It can only download or upload as fast as the connection it uses permits.

View System Information

You can view important system information with the System Profiler utility. System Profiler displays detailed reports about the state of your Macintosh. It provides important information about the hardware and software in your computer. You can use this information to help troubleshoot new hardware installations and upgrades. You can also retrieve the computer's serial number.

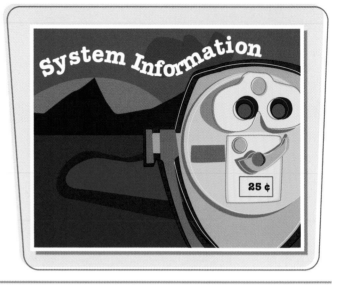

View System Information

LAUNCH SYSTEM PROFILER

① In the Finder, click (🍎).

② Click **About This Mac**.

The About This Mac window opens.

③ Click **More Info**.

FIND INSTALLED MEMORY

① In System Profiler, click **Hardware** to reveal its contents.

② Click **Memory**.

● System Profiler displays the memory slots in this computer and lists the amount of memory installed in each.

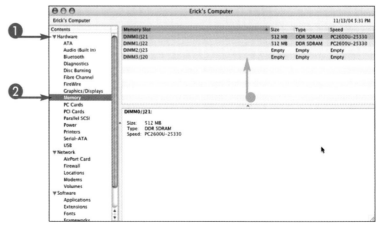

LOCATE SERIAL NUMBER AND CPU

1 In System Profiler, click **Hardware**.

● System Profiler displays the Hardware Overview, which includes the serial number, CPU type, and other system information for this computer.

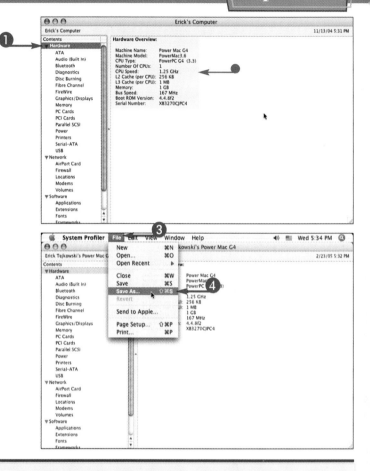

SAVE A SYSTEM PROFILER REPORT

1 Press ⌘ + 3 .

System Profiler displays a Full Profile.

3 Click **File**.

4 Click **Save As**.

The Save sheet opens.

5 Click **File Format** 🔃 and select **Rich Text Format**.

System Profiler saves the report as a Rich Text or Plain Text file that you can view with TextEdit.

TIPS

The serial number for my computer does not appear in the System Profiler report. Why?

Some Macintosh models do not support serial numbers in software. Those that do not will display a blank in the serial number field of System Profiler. You can still retrieve your serial number by looking at the serial number label on the rear or bottom of the machine.

How can System Profiler help me when I install new hardware?

System Profiler is a useful tool for troubleshooting hardware problems and installations. For example, when you install new RAM, check System Profiler upon restart. If the new RAM does not appear in the System Profiler report, the RAM could be installed improperly, may be incompatible with this machine, or may be defective. Good RAM installations should appear in the System Profiler report.

Erase and Repair Disks

At first glance, it may seem as though you cannot erase CDs in OS X, because the Finder does not support this operation. You can, however, erase CD-RWs with Disk Utility. You can also verify and repair disks and disk permissions on hard disks, CDs, and DVDs with Disk Utility.

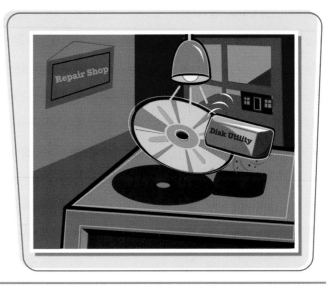

Erase and Repair Disks

LAUNCH DISK UTILITY

① In the Finder, press ⌘ + Shift + U .

The Utilities window opens.

② Double-click **Disk Utility**.

The Disk Utility application launches.

ERASE A CD

① In Disk Utility, insert a CD-RW that you want to erase.

② Control -click the CD-RW icon that appears in the Disk Utility window.

③ Click **Erase** in the contextual menu that opens.

An Erase window opens.

④ Click **Erase**.

Disk Utility erases the data from the CD.

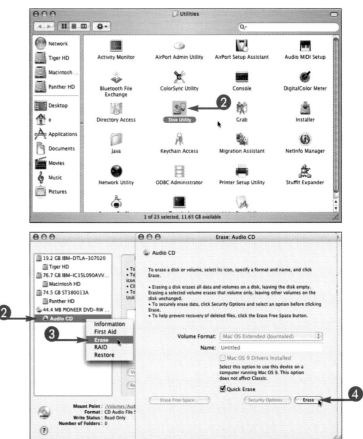

REPAIR DISK PERMISSIONS

1 In Disk Utility, select a disk.

2 Click the **FIRST AID** tab.

3 Click **Repair Disk Permissions**.

Disk Utility begins repairing any permissions errors on the disk.

REPAIR A DISK

1 In Disk Utility, click a disk.

2 Click the **FIRST AID** tab.

3 Click **Repair Disk**.

Disk Utility begins repairing any errors on the disk.

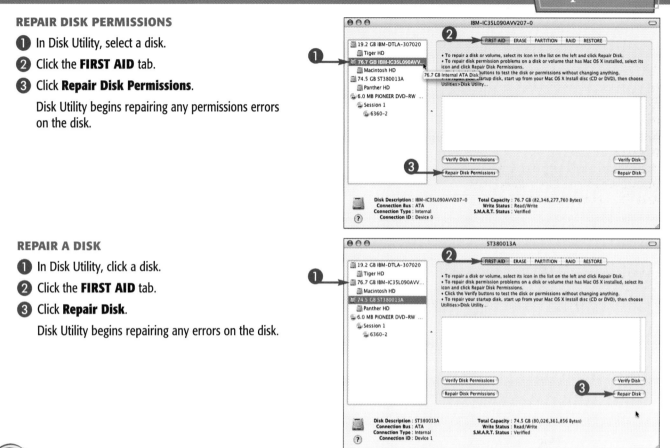

TIPS

Must I click Verify Disk before I click Repair Disk?

You do not have to verify a disk prior to repairing it. The repair process also performs verification. The verify option lets you know if the disk needs to be repaired or not, permitting you to defer the repair process if desired.

When should I repair a disk?

Any time that your computer shuts down unexpectedly, your disk is at risk of directory corruption. Some unexpected events include power outages and crashes. Some installers also cause disk directory corruption. Thus, it is a good idea to verify and repair your disk when your computer shuts down unexpectedly and after you run an installer, especially non-Apple installers.

Grab a Screen Shot

To capture TIFF screen shots of
your computer Desktop, you can
use the Grab utility included
with Mac OS X. You can also
grab PNG screen shots with a
few simple keystrokes that are
available in all applications.
When you take a screen shot,
you can grab the entire screen,
specific items on the screen, or
selected areas of the screen.

CAPTURE THE SCREEN WITH GRAB

1 Open the Utilities folder in the Applications folder.

2 Double-click **Grab** to launch it.

Grab launches.

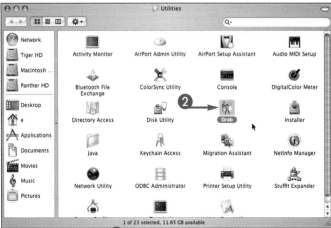

3 Click **Capture**.

4 Click **Screen**.

A window appears instructing you to click the mouse
to capture the screen.

⑤ Click the mouse.

Grab captures the screen and displays it.

You can save this image as a TIFF file for later viewing.

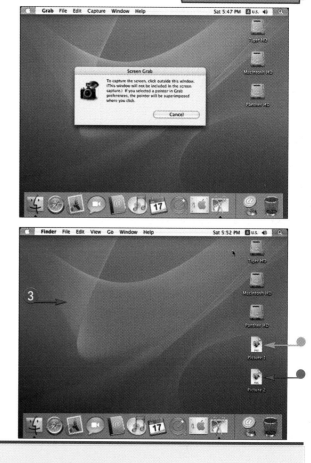

GRAB A SCREEN SHOT WITH A KEYSTROKE

① Press ⌘ + Shift + 3 .

● Your Mac plays the sound of a camera shutter and places a new PNG image file of the entire screen on the Desktop.

② Press ⌘ + Shift + 4 .

The cursor changes to cross hairs.

③ Click and drag to select a portion of the screen.

● The Mac places a new PNG image file of the selected region on the Desktop.

TIPS

Are there any other keyboard shortcuts for screen shots?

After you press ⌘ + Shift + 4 , press the Spacebar . The cursor changes to a camera. You can position that camera over any window, the Dock, an icon on the Desktop, or the menu bar to take a picture of only that element. As you move the camera cursor around the screen, interface elements appear highlighted. Click the desired element to grab a screen shot of it.

Can I save a screen shot to the Clipboard instead of a file?

Yes. To place a screen shot in the Clipboard, add the Control key to screen shot keyboard shortcuts. For example, ⌘ + Control + Shift + 3 captures the screen to the Clipboard. Once the screen shot is on the Clipboard, you can paste it into a document in any application that permits graphics by pressing ⌘ + V .

Dashboard is a collection of handy utilities that you can access with one keystroke from any application. You can use Dashboard utilities to display the time, check weather reports, use a calculator, read stock quotes, translate foreign languages, or even to play a game. When you have finished using Dashboard, you can dismiss it, again with only one key press.

Access Dashboard Utilities

ACTIVATE DASHBOARD

1 While using any application, press `F12`.

● The Dashboard layer opens obscuring all other windows and the Desktop.

2 Press `F12` again.

Dashboard disappears and returns you to the last application that you were using.

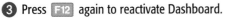

3 Press `F12` again to reactivate Dashboard.

4 Click the Dashboard circle icon with the "X" in it.

The Dashboard window grows, revealing other Dashboard Widgets.

USE A WIDGET

5 Click **World Clock**.

A World Clock Widget opens displaying the time.

6 Click **Settings** ().

The Widget flips around to reveal its settings on its rear surface.

7 Adjust the settings.

8 Click **Done**.

The Widget flips to reveal its front surface.

How can I remove a Widget from the Dashboard?

You can click and drag a Widget to the Dashboard Trash can to remove it from the Dashboard.

Can I install other Widgets?

You can download many different free Widgets on the Internet. One good place to start searching for Widgets is at The DashBoarder (www. thedashboarder.com). You can find Widgets of all sorts at the DashBoarder, including clocks, system utilities, games, educational tools, web camera utilities, and search engine interfaces.

Manage Printing

You can set up printers, perform routine maintenance, and monitor print jobs with the Printer Setup Utility. You can also set the default printer. During printing, you can use Printer Setup Utility to monitor the progress of print jobs, to pause queued jobs, or to cancel print jobs.

Manage Printing

SET THE DEFAULT PRINTER

① In the Finder, click **Go**.

② Click **Utilities**.

The Utilities window opens.

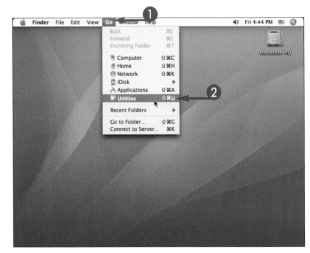

③ Double-click **Printer Setup Utility**.

The application launches.

④ Click a printer from the list of available printers.

This computer has one available printer shared on the network.

⑤ Click **Make Default**.

Printer Setup Utility designates that this printer as the default printer that appears in all print dialogs.

PAUSE, RESUME, OR CANCEL PRINTING

① Click a printer.

② Click **Printers**.

③ Click **Show Jobs**.

A window appears listing current print jobs.

④ Click a job that is having problems.

⑤ Click the desired printer action.

This example shows a print job being paused.

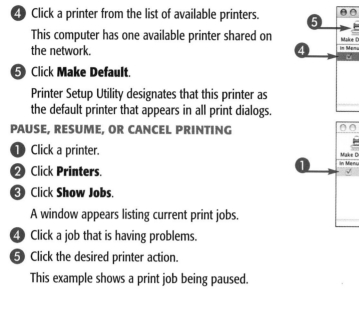

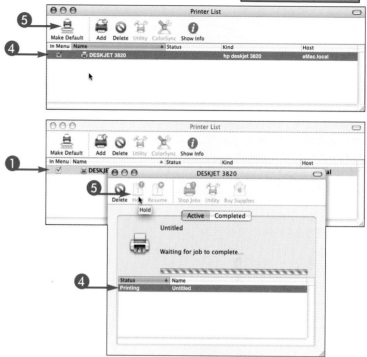

How do I cancel a print job completely?

If a printer has a paper jam, runs out of ink, or encounters some other trouble, you should stop the print job. Select the print job in the list of jobs and click the **Delete** icon at the top of the print window. If the printer was already printing a page, it will complete the task, immediately stop printing, and eject the page. You must open the document in its original application if you want to print it again.

What is a Desktop Printer and how do I create one?

A Desktop Printer is an icon on your Desktop that represents a printer connected either directly or via network to your computer. What makes this icon so useful is that you can drag multiple documents onto it in the Finder to print those documents. You can create a Desktop Printer by selecting the desired printer in Printer Setup Utility. Then, click **Create Desktop Printer** in the **Printers** menu.

The Terminal application is a tool that you use to issue text commands to the Mac. With the Terminal, you can perform tasks that would be time-consuming or impractical in the Finder. For example, you can list files on your hard drive and save that list in a text file, all with one command.

Issue Commands in the Terminal

① In the Finder, click **Go**.

② Click **Utilities**.

The Utilities folder opens.

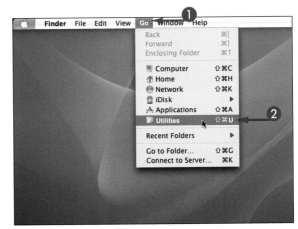

③ Double-click **Terminal**.

Terminal launches and opens a new terminal window.

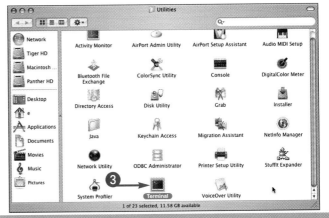

④ Type **ls** at the prompt and press Return .

Terminal lists the files in the current directory.

⑤ Type **cd ~/Desktop**.

Terminal changes the directory to the Desktop folder of the current user.

⑥ Type **ls**, which list files in a directory.

Terminal lists the files in the Desktop folder.

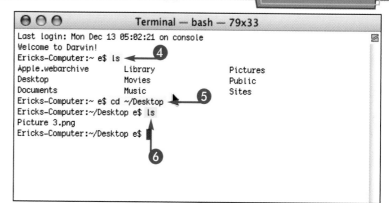

```
Terminal — bash — 79x33
Last login: Mon Dec 13 05:02:21 on console
Welcome to Darwin!
Ericks-Computer:~ e$ ls          ④
Apple.webarchive      Library        Pictures
Desktop               Movies         Public
Documents             Music          Sites
Ericks-Computer:~ e$ cd ~/Desktop    ⑤
Ericks-Computer:~/Desktop e$ ls
Picture 3.png
Ericks-Computer:~/Desktop e$
                                ⑥
```

SAVE COMMAND RESULTS TO A FILE

① Type **df -Hl**.

Terminal displays a list of the hard drives on this computer and valuable information about each one.

② Type **df -Hl > ~/Desktop/disks.txt** at the prompt.

Terminal runs the command and saves the output to a file named disks.txt on the Desktop.

③ Type **open ~/Desktop/disks.txt** at the prompt.

The disks.txt file opens in TextEdit.

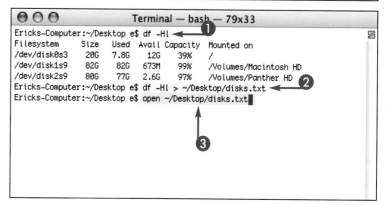

```
Terminal — bash — 79x33
Ericks-Computer:~/Desktop e$ df -Hl          ①
Filesystem      Size   Used   Avail Capacity  Mounted on
/dev/disk0s3    20G    7.8G   12G   39%        /
/dev/disk1s9    82G    82G    673M  99%        /Volumes/Macintosh HD
/dev/disk2s9    80G    77G    2.6G  97%        /Volumes/Panther HD
Ericks-Computer:~/Desktop e$ df -Hl > ~/Desktop/disks.txt    ②
Ericks-Computer:~/Desktop e$ open ~/Desktop/disks.txt
                                ③
```

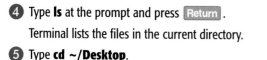

TIP

What are some other useful commands?

The **df** command tells you the free space on a drive. The **–Hl** option formats the output of the **df** command. **H** provides **K**, **M**, and **G** labels on the size of each disk. The **l** option causes the **df** command to display only locally mounted drives, excluding those on a network. **/** represents your computer. You can use the **man** command to display the documentation for any command. For example, in Terminal, type **man ls** to read the documentation for the **ls** command. Some common places where you can find commands are /bin, /sbin, /usr/bin, and /usr/sbin.

Automate Common Tasks

Mac OS X Tiger comes with a new tool called Automator that helps you to easily automate everyday tasks. You can perform a complex sequence of events, like creating an email message in Mail that lists important events from iCal and addresses the message to a group of recipients from Address Book. Moreover, you can perform sequences like this with drag-and-drop simplicity.

Automate Common Tasks

LAUNCH AUTOMATOR

1 Press ⌘ + Shift + A .

The Applications folder opens.

2 Double-click **Automator**.

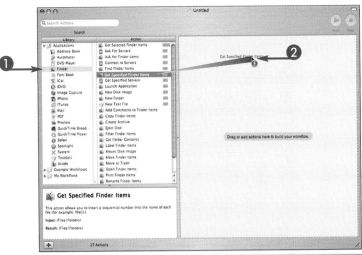

BUILD AN AUTOMATION WORKFLOW

1 In the Library, click **Finder**.

Automator displays the Actions pertinent to the Finder.

2 Click and drag **Get Specified Finder Items** to the Workflow space.

The **Get Specified Finder Items** action appears in the Workflow space.

CHOOSE WHICH IMAGE FILES TO PROCESS

③ Click ⊞.

An Open sheet appears giving you the chance to select files that you would like to process.

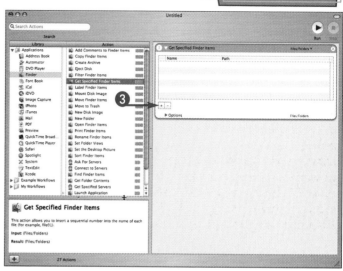

④ Click a JPEG image.

⑤ Click **Open**.

Automator adds the file to the action.

TIP

What is an Action?

An Action is an Automator building block that typically performs a single function. Automator has Actions that choose files, sort items in a list, apply effects to photos, and speak sentences, to name a few. Actions usually have an application associated with them, since that is where you normally perform those functions (for example, Mail Actions for composing a message, addressing recipients, and sending a message).

continued

After you create a Workflow and add images to it, you can make copies of the images with a new action in your Workflow, so you do not alter the originals. Then, you can a grayscale filter Action to the Workflow, which will convert photographs from color to black and white. Finally, with Actions in place, you can run the Workflow to perform the desired task.

Automate Common Tasks *(continued)*

COPY IMAGE FILES

⑥ Drag **Copy Finder Items** to add it to the Workflow.

This action makes a copy of the files from the first action, places them on the Desktop, and passes them onto the next action.

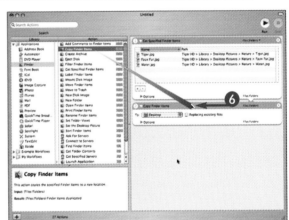

APPLY A GRAYSCALE FILTER TO EACH IMAGE

⑦ Click **Preview**.

⑧ Drag **Apply ColorSync Profile to Images** to the Workflow.

Automator adds the action to the Workflow.

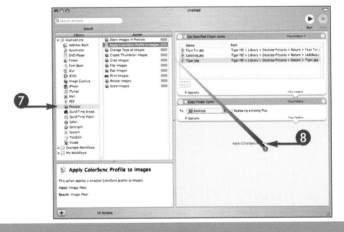

9 Click **Profile** and select **Abstract**.

10 Click **Gray Tone**.

This ColorSync Profile converts a color image to grayscale.

11 Click **Run** ().

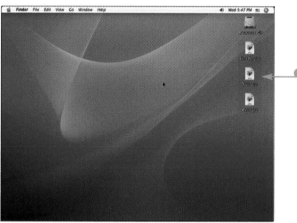

● Automator creates copies of the image files on the Desktop and applies a grayscale filter to each.

TIPS

Can I use an Automator workflow without launching Automator?
You can save a workflow as a stand-alone application by clicking **Save As** in the File menu and selecting **Application** in the File Format pop-up menu of the Save dialog box. To launch the saved application, simply double-click it.

How do I remove a step from the workflow?
Click the step to select it and press **Delete** to remove it from the workflow. When you delete a step from the workflow, you disconnect any steps that appear before or after the deleted step. You must reconnect these two steps to continue using them as part of the workflow.

Connecting Peripherals to a Mac

Peripherals are external devices that you can connect to your Macintosh, such as a digital camera or iPod music player, that extend the functionality of your Mac. With Mac OS X, you can attach a wide variety of peripherals to your Mac. Tiger also gives you some useful software to help you get the most out of the peripherals.

iMovie HD offers a new feature called Magic iMovie, which helps you to automatically create an iMovie from a digital camcorder. All you have to do is connect a video camera to your Mac and adjust a few settings. iMovie takes care of the rest.

Make a Magic iMovie

1 Connect a FireWire video camera to your Mac.

2 Click **iMovie HD**.

The iMovie HD application launches.

3 Click **Make a Magic iMovie**.

The Create Project window opens.

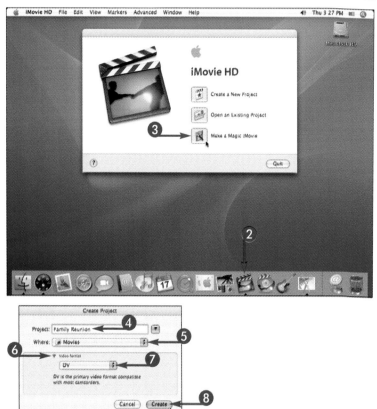

4 Name the project.

5 Click ◈ and select a location for the project on your hard drive.

6 Click the **Video Format** triangle.

The triangle should be pointing downward.

7 Click ◈ and select **DV**.

DV is the most common video format for digital camcorders.

8 Click **Create**.

iMovie creates a Magic iMovie project.

⑨ Type a name for the movie.

⑩ Click **Use** (☐ changes to ☑).

⑪ Click ⊟ and select the **Cross Dissolve** transition.

⑫ Click **Play a music soundtrack** (☐ changes to ☑).

⑬ Click **Choose Music** to select music.

⑭ Click **Send to iDVD** (☐ changes to ☑).

When checked, this option causes iMovie to transfer a completed Magic iMovie to iDVD where you can burn a DVD.

⑮ Click **Create**.

iMovie creates a Magic iMovie, importing footage, adding transitions and background music, and titling the movie.

Note: See Chapter 7 to read more about iMovie editing once iMovie finishes creating the Magic iMovie.

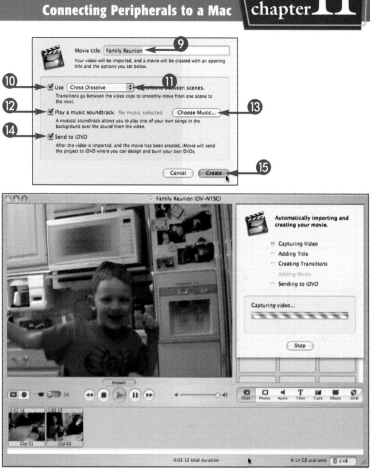

TIPS

What can I do with a Magic iMovie once iMovie finishes creating it?

You can do anything with a Magic iMovie that you would normally do with any other iMovie. You can share the movie with others over email or the Web or burn it on a DVD. A Magic iMovie project is really no different than a typical iMovie project, except that iMovie takes care of preparing the media and project elements for you. In a traditional iMovie project, you must import footage, add transitions and sound, and title the movie manually. Magic iMovie handles these tasks for you automatically. For details, see Chapter 7.

Magic iMovie added some footage that I do not want in my movie. Can I remove it and edit other elements of the project?

If you do not like how some aspect of a Magic iMovie looks or sounds, you can edit it manually just as you would edit any other iMovie project. You can remove clips, choose different soundtrack music, or change transitions. See Chapter 7 for more information.

Copy Music to an iPod

iTunes is the perfect match for the iPod. You can use iTunes to transfer songs from your Mac to an iPod. Further, iTunes can sync its library with your iPod, so you have the same songs in both. The iPod is also compatible with iTunes playlists, so you can keep your music organized wherever you go.

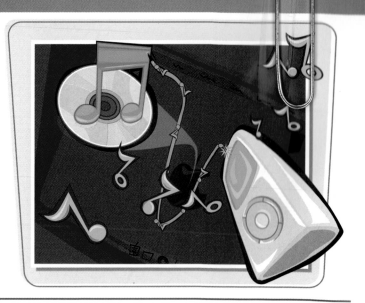

Copy Music to an iPod

① Click the **iTunes** icon in the Dock.

The iTunes window appears.

② Plug the iPod into the FireWire port on your Macintosh and turn it on.

● The iPod appears in the iTunes Source list.

Note: *If this is the first time you have used the iPod with iTunes, iTunes automatically syncs the iPod.*

③ ⌘-click **iPod**.

④ Click **iPod Options**.

The iPod Preferences window opens.

⑤ Click **iPod.**

⑥ Click **Automatically update all songs and playlists** (○ changes to ◉).

You can deactivate automatic syncing by clicking **Manually manage songs and playlists** (○ changes to ◉).

⑦ Click **OK**.

iTunes syncs the songs in your iTunes library with the music on your iPod.

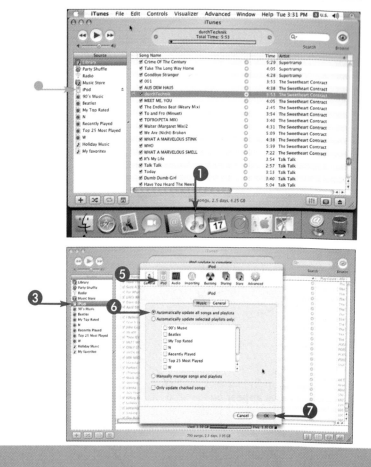

EJECT THE IPOD

1️⃣ Click the **Eject iPod** button.

iTunes ejects the iPod.

2️⃣ Power down the iPod and disconnect it from your Mac.

1️⃣

TIPS

What Preferences option should I choose if I do not want my entire iTunes library on my iPod?

In the iPod Preferences, click **Manually manage songs and playlists** (○ changes to ●) to manually select the music that you want on your iPod. This prevents iTunes from automatically syncing with your iPod. In the main iTunes interface, click and drag songs from the Library to the iPod in the **Source** list. The new songs appear on the iPod.

How do I tell iTunes to open every time I connect an iPod to my computer?

In the iPod pane of the iTunes Preferences window, click the **Open iTunes when attached** option (☐ changes to ☑). iTunes now launches each time you connect an iPod to your Mac.

Save Files from an iPod in the Finder

In addition to iTunes, an iPod is right at home in the Finder. Because an iPod can act like any other hard drive, you can save files on it just like you do on your Mac's hard drive. This makes the iPod ideal for transferring large files between two computers, like those at work and home.

Save Files from an iPod in the Finder

CONNECT AN IPOD

① Plug an iPod into the FireWire port on your Macintosh.

An icon representing the iPod appears on the Desktop.

② Double-click the **iPod** icon.

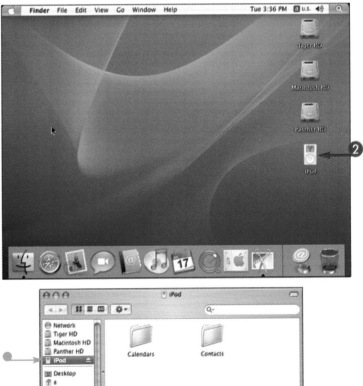

● A window opens displaying the contents of the iPod.

③ In the Sidebar of a Finder window, click **Documents**.

④ Click and drag files from the iPod to the Documents folder in your Home folder on your hard drive.

The Finder copies the files to your hard drive.

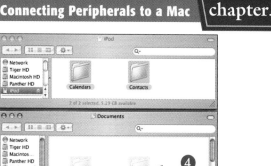

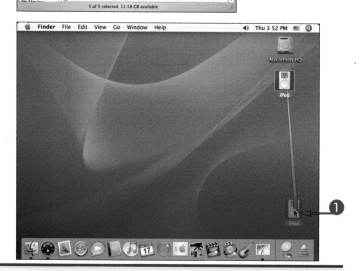

DISCONNECT THE IPOD

① Click and drag the **iPod** icon on the Desktop to the Trash icon on the Dock.

As you drag the iPod icon in the Finder, the Trash icon in the Dock changes to an Eject icon.

The iPod ejects when you drop it on the Eject icon.

② Power down the iPod and disconnect it from your Macintosh.

TIPS

Can I use my iPod for anything else besides file storage?

Because the iPod operates much like any other hard drive, you can perform any task with it that you might perform with any other hard drive. For example, you can install an operating system on your iPod and use it to start up any Mac in an emergency. iPods are not designed to handle the heat of constant use that an operating system requires, but they can work for short periods of time as an emergency startup disk. You can also run the usual Disk Utility diagnostic tests and repairs on an iPod drive.

Can I delete files from an iPod through the Finder?

To delete files from an iPod drive, begin by connecting the iPod to your computer. An iPod icon appears on the Desktop. Double-click the **iPod** icon on the Desktop to view its contents. Then, click and drag the files from the iPod to the Trash just as you would drag files from any other drive or disk.

Printers are among the most common Mac OS X peripherals. The printing functions in Mac OS X are top notch. You can adjust a multitude of print settings in Mac OS X Tiger to produce high-quality printed documents. You can change the number of copies you want to print, the quality of the print job, the orientation of the paper, the printer you want to use, and many other settings.

Print Documents

ADJUST PAGE SETTINGS

1 Open a document in any application that supports printing.

2 Click **File**.

3 Click **Page Setup**.

The Page Setup sheet opens.

You can adjust the paper size, page orientation, and other settings specific to your printer and the job you wish to print.

4 Click **Settings** to change page attributes and custom paper sizes.

5 Click ⬦ and select a printer.

● If needed, set the **Paper Size**, **Orientation**, and **Scale** options to change how the printed page looks.

6 Click **OK** to accept the settings.

The Page Setup sheet closes.

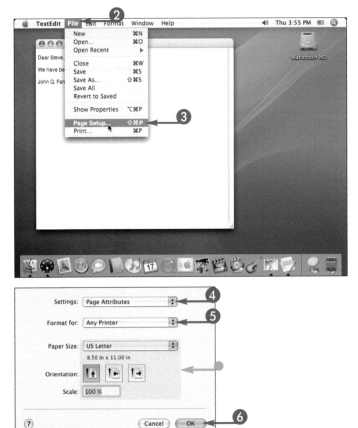

PRINT A DOCUMENT

① Open a document in any application that supports printing.

② Click **File**.

③ Click **Print**.

The Print settings sheet opens.

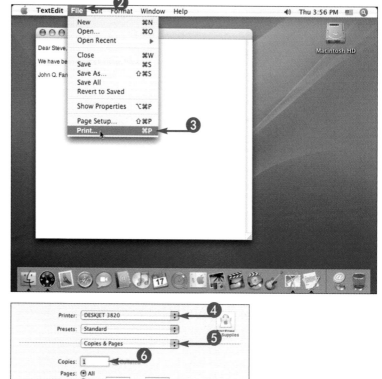

④ Click and select a printer.

⑤ Click and select **Copies & Pages**.

⑥ Type in the number of copies you want to print.

The default value is **1**.

⑦ Click **Print**.

The printer begins printing the document.

TIP

How do I set up new printers?
Use Printer Setup Utility, located in the Utilities folder, to set up new printers. You can set up various types of printers to work with Tiger, including USB, FireWire, and Ethernet printers. You can also connect to network printers and those that work with Microsoft Windows and UNIX computers.

Mount a Laptop as a Disk Drive

Macs have a disk operation called Target Disk Mode that permits you to connect two Macs together, so that one of the Macs displays the other Mac's hard drive on its Desktop. Because of portability, this is especially useful for laptop owners. You can connect a laptop to a desktop computer at home or the office to transfer files between the two.

Mount a Laptop as a Disk Drive

ACTIVATE TARGET DISK MODE

① On the computer that you want to use as a target disk, click **System Preferences**.

The System Preferences window opens.

② Click **Startup Disk**.

The Startup Disk pane opens.

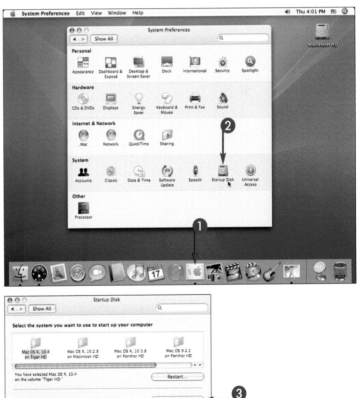

③ Click **Target Disk Mode**.

The computer reboots in Target Disk Mode.

④ Plug a FireWire cable into a FireWire port on the computer in Target Disk Mode and connect the other end of the cable to a FireWire port on another Mac.

● When the laptop finishes booting, its drive appears on the Desktop of the other computer.

TIP

What benefit does Target Disk Mode have over a traditional Ethernet network connection?

Although an Ethernet connection can also permit you to transfer files between two Macs, Target Disk Mode is much faster at performing the task. For small files, Target Disk Mode may not be worth the effort, particularly if you already have an Ethernet network. If you need to transfer very large files, however, Target Disk Mode performs the transfer more quickly.

Fax a Document

Mac OS X features full fax capabilities. You can fax documents using the built-in modem in your computer from practically any application that supports printing. OS X converts the document to a printed fax document and transmits it over the telephone lines to another fax machine. The OS X fax software also handles cover pages.

Fax a Document

① Open a file in an application that supports printing.

② Click **File**.

③ Click **Print**.

The Print sheet opens.

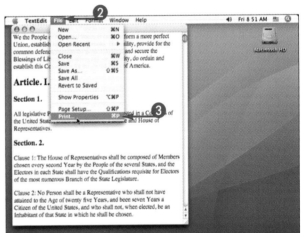

④ Click **Fax**.

The Fax settings sheet appears.

⑤ Click **Fax PDF**.

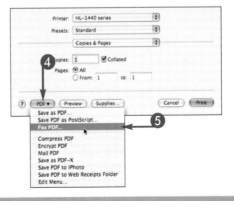

6 Type a telephone number in the To field.

7 Click **Fax**.

Mac OS X faxes the document.

To:	
Dialing Prefix:	
Modem:	No Fax Selected
Presets:	Standard
	Item 1

Preview   Cancel Fax

A status window shows how many pages of the fax has been transmitted and whether the fax was successfully received.

● You can click **Stop Jobs** if you need to cancel the fax job.

Internal Modem

Delete Hold Resume Stop Jobs Utility

Untitled

Connected to 1-317-572-4306

Status	Name	Fax Number
Faxing	Untitled	1-317-572-4306

TIPS

Can I fax documents from any application?

You can fax documents from any application that supports printing. TextEdit and iPhoto are common choices for sending faxes, as they contain text information or scanned images that people often want to fax. Because the fax features are part of the print dialog, they are always instantly accessible.

Can I use the phone numbers in my Address Book to send a fax?

Yes, you can use the telephone numbers stored in Address Book to send a fax. In the Fax settings window, click the Address Book button to the right side of the To field. An Address Book window opens where you can choose a fax number to dial.

Using a Microphone with iChat

Chatting on the Internet has always been fun, but for some, typing was always a hindrance to good conversations. With iChat and a microphone, you can talk to as many as nine of your iChat buddies much like you would on a telephone. Aside from the price of your Internet connection, there is no additional cost to speak with friends through iChat using a microphone.

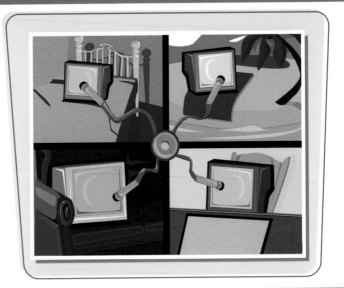

Using a Microphone with iChat

CONNECT A MICROPHONE TO YOUR MAC

① Connect a microphone to the USB, FireWire, or built-in audio jack on your Macintosh computer.

If you have a built-in microphone, you can use that too.

SET UP ICHAT AUDIO

① Click **iChat** in the Dock to launch it.

② Click **iChat**.

③ Click **Preferences**.

The iChat Preferences window opens.

④ Click **Video**.

⑤ Click 🔽 and select your microphone.

⑥ Click 🔲.

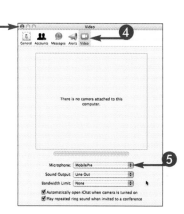

TALK TO ICHAT BUDDIES WITH AUDIO

① Press ⌘ + ① to open the Buddy List.

② Click a Buddy that has a telephone or camera icon next to his or her name.

③ Click the **Telephone** icon.

● iChat initiates an audio connection.

TIP

What kind of microphones can I use with iChat?

You can use almost any kind of microphone with iChat, as long as you have the proper hardware to interface with that microphone. Some computers, like iBooks, PowerBooks, iMacs, and eMacs, have built-in microphones that will suffice for iChat conversations. If your computer does not have a built-in microphone, you can plug in a microphone to a built-in audio input jack on the back or side of your computer. If you do not have a built-in audio input, you may need to purchase an external audio interface that connects to either USB or FireWire. Because iChat is also video-compatible, you can also use the built-in microphone on some video and Web cameras, including the iSight.

Conduct a Video Chat

Welcome to the future! You can use iChat to converse with up to three friends at once using live video. Connect a camera to your Mac, launch iChat, and within seconds you can video conference with others across the globe.

Conduct a Video Chat

CONNECT A VIDEO CAMERA TO YOUR MAC

① Connect a video camera to the FireWire jack on your Macintosh.

② Turn on the video camera.

SET UP ICHAT VIDEO

③ Click **iChat** in the Dock to launch it.

④ Click **iChat**.

⑤ Click **Preferences**.

The iChat Preferences window opens.

6 Click **Video**.

7 Click a camera.

8 Click an audio source.

9 Click **Close**.

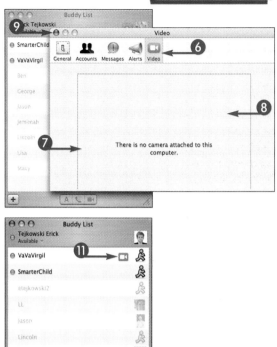

TALK TO ICHAT BUDDIES OVER VIDEO

10 Press ⌘+1 to open the Buddy List.

11 Click a buddy's camera icon ().

iChat initiates a video connection.

What kind of cameras can I use with iChat?

iChat requires a video camera that has a FireWire connection. Some common FireWire cameras are Apple's iSight and MiniDV video camcorders. iChat is made with iSight in mind, so you can access iSight-specific settings directly in iChat. MiniDV cameras often require you to remove any videotape from the machine and to set the camera to Camera Mode to use it with iChat.

Can I conduct a one-way video chat?

iChat does not require both participants in a chat to have video to use it. If only one user has a video source, the video chat sessions works in a similar fashion, but only one participant will be able to view video. The user with a video source will see no video icon for the user that does not have a video source. The user without a video source can, however, continue to chat using an audio source if one is available.

Retrieve Pictures from a Camera in the Finder

You can view digital cameras in the Finder and transfer files from the camera to your hard drive. A camera icon appears on the Desktop just like any other drive. From there you can copy files from the camera to a location such as the Pictures folder on your hard drive. After you copied files from the camera to your Mac, power down and disconnect the camera from your computer.

Retrieve Pictures from a Camera in the Finder

PLUG IN A CAMERA

① Connect a camera to your Macintosh.

This example shows a camera connected via USB cable.

An icon representing the camera appears on the Desktop.

② Click **File**.

③ Click **New Finder Window**.

A new Finder window opens.

④ Click the camera icon in the window's Sidebar.

A folder displays the images stored on the camera.

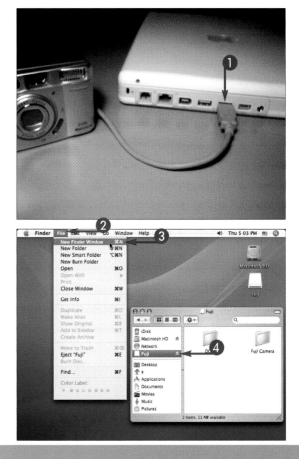

COPY PICTURES FROM THE CAMERA

① Drag images from the camera's window to a folder on your hard drive.

This example shows images dragged to the Pictures folder.

The Finder copies the files to your hard drive.

The original images remain in the camera.

DISCONNECT THE CAMERA

① Drag the camera icon from the Desktop to the Trash.

● The Trash icon changes to an Eject icon and the camera drive disappears from view.

② Power down and disconnect the camera from your Macintosh.

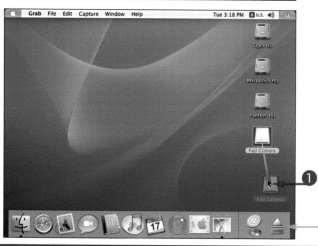

TIPS

What if the drive for the camera does not appear on the Desktop?

If the drive does not appear on the Desktop, and iPhoto launches instead, open the Preferences window in the Image Capture application and click the Camera tab. In the Camera tab, click **No application** in the only pop-up menu. Click **OK** to dismiss the Preferences window. A camera icon should now appear on the Desktop when you connect a camera to your Mac.

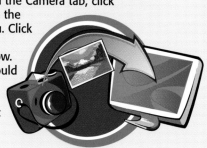

Can I delete images on my camera from the Finder?

Yes. Connect a camera to your Mac. To delete files from a camera drive on the Desktop, simply click and drag the image files from the camera to the Trash icon. Empty the Trash to make the deletion complete, just as you would delete any other files. You can also perform **Get Info** operations on image files in a camera by selecting an image file and pressing ⌘+⎵.

iDVD has a useful new feature for burning video to disc without any hassles. With the OneStep DVD feature, iDVD imports footage from a camcorder and burns the results to DVD as an auto-play movie. No other attention is required from a human to produce professional results.

Create a OneStep DVD

① Connect a digital camcorder to your Macintosh.

Note: See your camcorder literature for proper connection instructions.

② Click **iDVD**.

The iDVD application launches.

③ Click **OneStep DVD**.

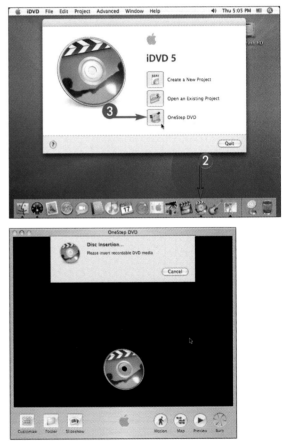

iDVD prompts you to insert a blank DVD.

④ Put a blank disc into the machine and close the DVD drive door.

iDVD begins the process of capturing footage from the camera, preparing the DVD, and burning the result to disc.

● These indicators display the status of the process.

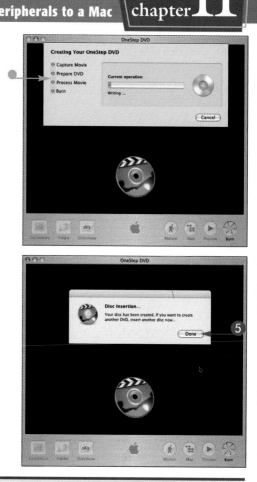

When iDVD completes the DVD, it ejects the disc and prompts you with a message to let you know the process is complete.

To burn another disc, place it in the DVD drive.

⑤ Click **Done**.

The OneStep process sounds simple enough, but surely I must have to rewind the tape before creating a OneStep DVD?

iDVD can remotely control many FireWire DV camcorders, so it is often not even necessary to rewind the tape before creating a OneStep DVD. iDVD will rewind the tape for you before importing footage from it. iDVD will also stop the tape when it finishes importing footage from the camera.

Does iDVD add a menu or any other features to OneStep DVDs?

OneStep DVDs are plain video DVDs. They contain no menus, chapters, or navigation like other iDVD projects do. They simply contain the unedited video footage from your video camera. OneStep DVDs are great for archiving video footage and for simple video projects. You will want to use the features found in a full-fledged iDVD project for any projects that are more complex.

12

Troubleshooting Mac Problems

Although Macintosh computers are solid and reliable machines, they may still fall victim to a variety of maladies that can make your computing experience less than satisfactory. You can perform some simple steps to help keep your Mac running smoothly.

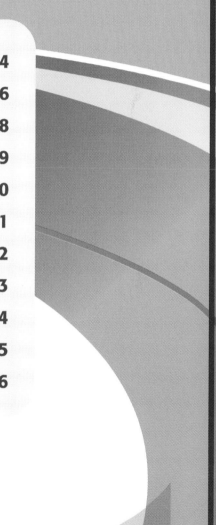

Unfreeze a Frozen Application

Sometimes applications may not behave as expected. When an application freezes or stops operating properly, you can force it to quit without restarting your computer. You can quit an application from the Force Quit Applications window or from the Dock. After you force quit an application, you can continue working with other applications uninterrupted.

FORCE QUIT A FROZEN APPLICATION

① Press ⌘ + Option + Esc .

The Force Quit Applications window opens with frozen applications appearing red.

② Click **Force Quit**.

A sheet opens asking you to confirm that you want to force quit the application.

If you need to force quit the Finder, then a Relaunch button appears instead.

③ Click **Force Quit**.

The application quits.

FORCE QUIT FROM THE DOCK

1 Press and hold **Option**.

2 Click and hold the mouse cursor on an application icon in the Dock.

A contextual menu opens.

Running applications have a small triangle beneath their icons in the Dock.

3 Click **Force Quit**.

The application quits.

● The triangle vanishes, indicating that the application is no longer running.

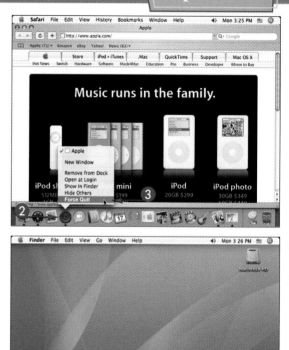

TIPS

Is it safe to force quit an application?

When you force quit an application, any work that you had not saved in that application will be lost. Otherwise, you can usually quit an application without affecting its subsequent performance. One exception, however, relates to preference files. If an application is in the middle of opening or creating a preferences file when it crashes, the application may not operate properly later. The remedy is simple — delete the preferences file located in ~/Library/Preferences.

What causes applications to freeze? Is it my fault?

Applications may freeze due to programming bugs that are caused by the people who created the application. Other times, a crash or freeze may stem from interplay between two or more applications that the creators did not envision happening. If the software is working properly, it should not crash or freeze; and a user cannot be blamed for these problems.

Update Mac OS System Software

As the Mac OS evolves, Apple releases updates to the software. You can install system software updates using the System Preferences. The Software Update feature contacts Apple to discover what updates are available and displays that list for you. Once the update mechanism is initiated, the software downloads the latest updates directly from Apple and installs them on your computer.

Update Mac OS System Software

1. Click .
2. Click **System Preferences**.

   System Preferences opens.

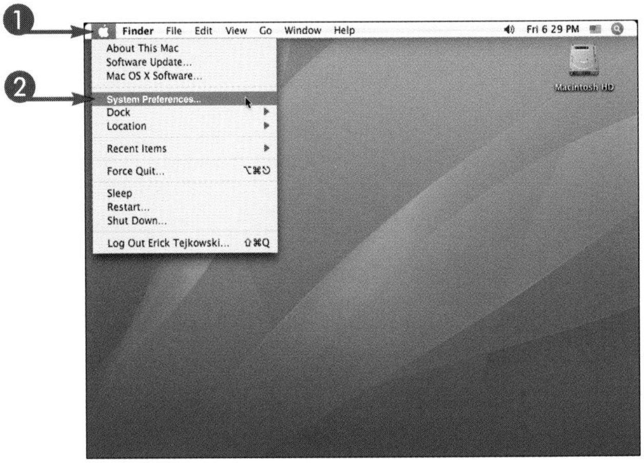

3. Click **Software Update**.

   The Software Update pane opens.

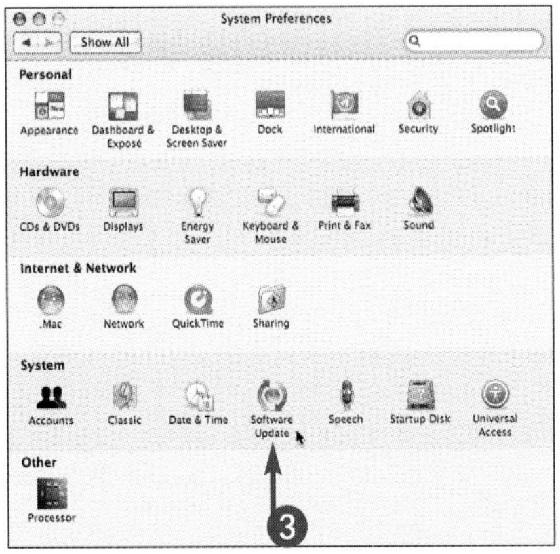

④ Click **Check for updates** (☐ changes to ☑).

⑤ Click ⬍ and select an interval from the drop-down menu.

This example tells Software Update to automatically check the Internet for new or updated software on a weekly basis.

⑥ Click **Check Now**.

● Software Update checks the Internet for new or updated software.

If I set Software Update to check for updates automatically, will it install software without asking me?

No. Although Software Update can check automatically for updates, it asks you to confirm installation before installing anything on your hard drive. You can also tell Software Update to download the files automatically in the background, so they are available for you to install when you feel like it. Software Update then downloads the software from Apple's servers and stores the update package on your hard drive for later installation. At no time does Software Update install anything on your computer without you first telling it to do so.

The updates take a long time to download. Is there anything I can do to lessen this wait?

When you have numerous updates to install on your computer, it can take a long time to download the software before you can even install it. You can set Software Update to automatically download updates in the background as they become available, so you can install the software later without having to wait for the updates to download. This is also a useful feature for laptop users who may not always have network access.

When you update your system
software, you may encounter
software that you do not need.
You can tell Software Update to
ignore updates that you do not
want to use.

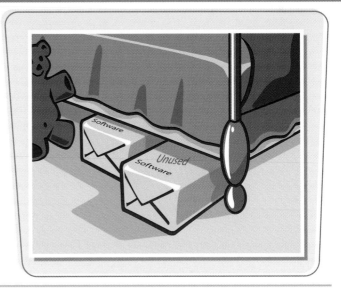

Disable an Update

1 In the System Preferences, click **Software Update**.

Note: *To launch System Preferences, see Chapter 3.*

The Software Update pane opens.

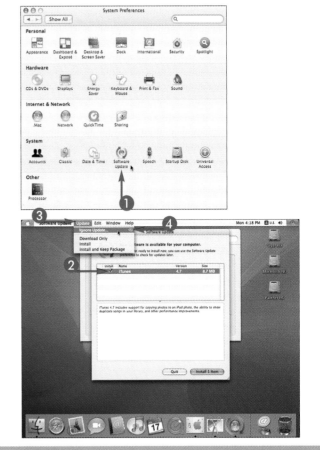

2 Click **Install** (☐ changes to ☑) for any updates
that you do not want to use.

3 Click **Update**.

4 Click **Ignore Update**.

Software Update ignores this update.

You may not use all applications that are
installed on your Mac. You can uninstall
applications quickly and easily without
affecting other software. Uninstalling an
application can free up extra disk space.
It can also help prevent conflicts between
multiple versions of the same application,
where double-clicking a document icon
causes the wrong version of an
application to launch.

Uninstall an Application

① In the Finder, click **Go**.

② Click **Applications**.

The Applications folder opens.

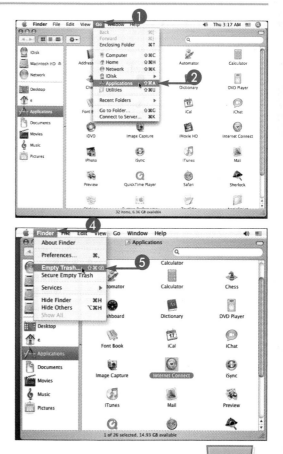

③ Click and drag an application that you want to
uninstall to the Trash.

④ Click **Finder**.

⑤ Click **Empty Trash**.

The Finder deletes the application.

Repair Permissions

Because Mac OS X is a multiuser environment, each file and folder on the hard drive has a set of assigned permissions that describes who can read, write, or, in the case of an application, execute the file. Sometimes a Mac misbehaves when these permissions are set incorrectly. You can repair permissions to prevent program problems.

Repair Permissions

① Press ⌘ + Shift + U.

The Utilities folder opens.

② Double-click **Disk Utility** to launch it.

The Disk Utility window appears.

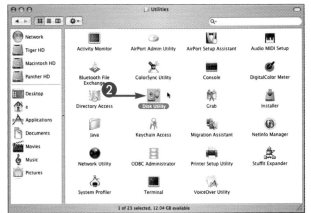

③ Click a disk to select it.

④ Click the **First Aid** tab.

⑤ Click **Repair Disk Permissions**.

Disk Utility begins scanning the disk and repairing any permissions errors it finds.

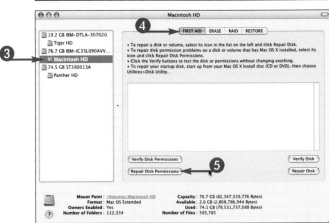

The hard drive in a Macintosh is a complex and high precision mechanism. As a result, hard drives can malfunction and cause improper operation of your Mac. You can repair some hard drive problems with Disk Utility. Chief among the errors that Disk Utility can fix are disk permissions and the directory structure. The directory structure describes where files reside on a disk. Permissions determine who can access folders and files on a disk.

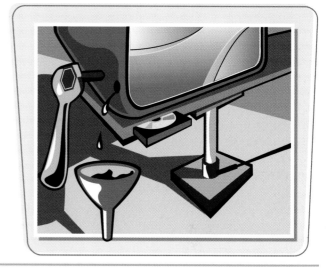

Repair a Disk

① Press ⌘ + **Shift** + **U**.

The Utilities folder opens.

② Double-click **Disk Utility** to launch it.

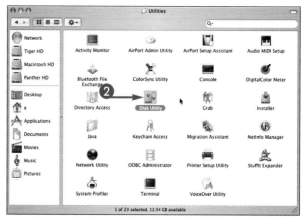

③ In the Disk Utility window, select a disk.

④ Click the **First Aid** tab.

⑤ Click **Repair Disk**.

Disk Utility begins verifying and repairing any problems it finds on the disk.

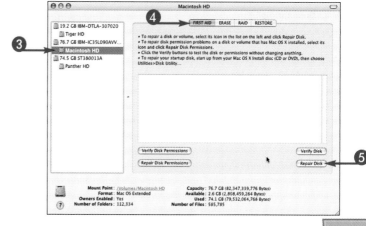

Change Your Password

As a precaution, security experts recommend that you periodically change your account password. Changing the password helps stop unauthorized users from accessing your machine, particularly if they know your current password. You can change your password in the Accounts pane of the System Preferences by typing your current password and then typing and confirming your new password. You can also enter a password hint to help you remember the password later.

Change Your Password

1 Click System Preferences in the Dock.

2 Click **Accounts**.

The Accounts pane appears.

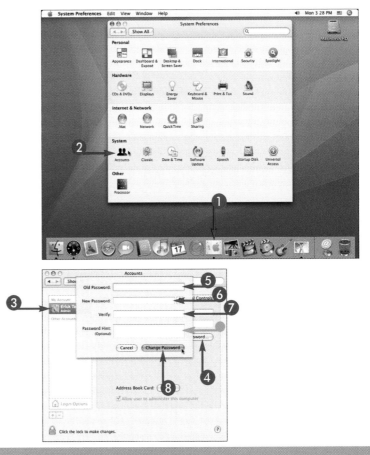

3 Click your account.

4 Click **Change Password**.

5 Type your previous password.

6 Type your new password.

7 Type your new password again.

● Type an optional hint to help you remember the password.

8 Click **Change Password**.

The System Preferences window closes and the new password is now functional.

You can press different key combinations when your computer starts up to change the startup procedure. One combination forces your Mac to start from a CD or DVD, while the other causes your computer to start in Safeboot mode. These startup keyboard combinations are useful for troubleshooting some system problems and for installing Mac OS X operating systems.

In Safeboot mode, the Mac reboots and temporarily disables login items and other nonessential system software.

Employ Startup Tricks

START FROM A CD OR DVD

① Insert a CD or DVD that contains an operating system into your Mac.

If you are installing a Mac OS X operating system, the CD or DVD will contain a valid operating system.

② Click 🍎.

③ Click **Restart**.

④ As the computer restarts, press and hold C.

The computer boots from the CD or DVD.

START IN SAFEBOOT MODE

① Click 🍎.

② Click **Restart**.

③ As the computer restarts, press and hold Shift.

If your computer restarts and operates properly, you may have need to disable items in the Login Items pane of the System Preferences.

Note: See Chapter 3 for more information on System Preferences.

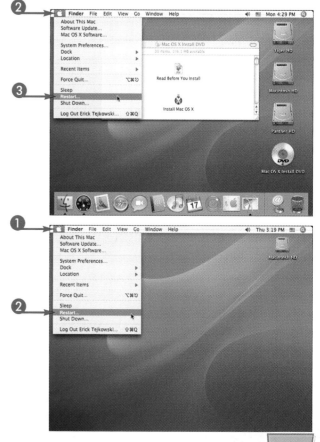

Stop Classic Mode

Classic Mode on Mac OS X permits you to run applications from Mac OS 9. It is not the most elegant part of OS X, but it can help you if you need access to an old application. If you continue to use Classic Macintosh applications, you can sometimes experience unusual system performance in OS X when the OS 9 Classic side of the operating system begins misbehaving. You can force quit Classic Mode in the System Preferences.

Stop Classic Mode

① Click **System Preferences** in the Dock.

The System Preferences window opens.

② Click **Classic**.

The Classic pane opens.

③ Click the **Start/Stop** tab.

④ Select the system folder that contains the version of Classic that you want to stop.

This will probably be your startup drive.

⑤ Click **Stop**.

Classic Mode stops running.

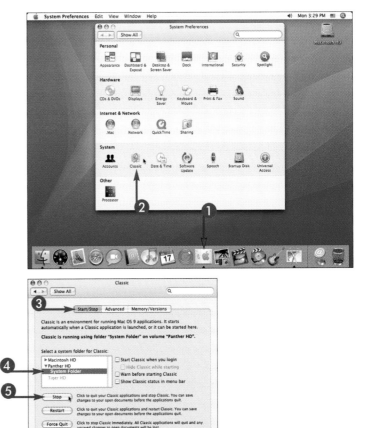

When your computer becomes so troublesome that you do not know what else to do to fix it, you should consider creating a new user. You can operate your computer as this new user to determine whether the original user's settings are causing the problems. If the new user does not exhibit the same problems, you can safely assume that something is wrong with the user account and not the computer in general.

Troubleshoot with a New User

① Click **System Preferences** in the Dock.

The System Preferences window appears.

② Click **Accounts**.

The Accounts pane opens.

③ Click ➕.

The Accounts pane guides you through the new user process.

④ Log out and then log back in as the new user.

If your computer operates properly while you are using the new account, your previous account may be the source of the problem.

Fix Corrupt Preference Files

Applications typically save information in preference files for later use. These files can also become corrupt if there is a bug in the software that creates them or if a crash causes the file to not be updated properly. You can sometimes fix application problems by removing an errant preference file and restarting the application.

Fix Corrupt Preference Files

Note: The Safari application is not functioning properly in this example.

① In the Finder, press ⌘ + Shift + H .

The current user's Home folder opens.

② Double-click **Library**.

③ Double-click **Preferences**.

The Preferences folder opens.

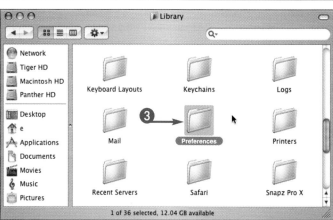

④ Drag the preference file for the problematic application to the Trash.

Preference files usually follow a naming scheme **com.vendor.appname.plist**. For example, the Safari preference file has the name **com.apple.safari.plist**.

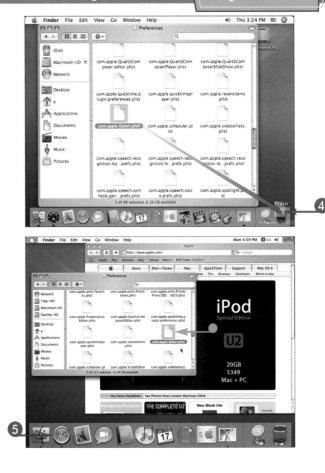

⑤ Relaunch the application that uses the missing preference file.

● A new preference file appears in place of the deleted file.

TIP

Is it safe to remove a preference file from the Preferences folder?

In most situations, removing a preference file will not cause software to malfunction. However, it may result in the loss of your settings for that application. If you are uncertain whether the application will work properly after removing a preference file, back up the preference file instead of dragging it to the Trash. To create a backup of the preference file, press **Option** and drag the preference file from the Preferences folder to the Desktop. A new copy of the file appears on the Desktop. Now, it is safe to delete the preference file in the Preferences folder. Later, you can restore the preference file by dragging it from the Desktop folder to the Preferences folder.

Index

Index

Index

Index

Index